M000190890

Candles in the Dark

Successful Organizations in Pakistan's
Weak Institutional Environment

Mahmood Ali Ayub

and

Syed Turab Hussain

OXFORD
UNIVERSITY PRESS

OXFORD
UNIVERSITY PRESS

Oxford University Press is a department of the University of Oxford.
It furthers the University's objective of excellence in research, scholarship,
and education by publishing worldwide. Oxford is a registered trade mark of
Oxford University Press in the UK and in certain other countries

Published in Pakistan by
Ameena Saiyid, Oxford University Press
No.38, Sector 15, Korangi Industrial Area,
PO Box 8214, Karachi-74900, Pakistan

© Oxford University Press 2016

The moral rights of the author have been asserted

First Edition published in 2016

All rights reserved. No part of this publication may be reproduced, stored in
a retrieval system, or transmitted, in any form or by any means, without the
prior permission in writing of Oxford University Press, or as expressly permitted
by law, by licence, or under terms agreed with the appropriate reprographics
rights organization. Enquiries concerning reproduction outside the scope of the
above should be sent to the Rights Department, Oxford University Press, at the
address above

You must not circulate this work in any other form
and you must impose this same condition on any acquirer

ISBN 978-0-19-940336-3

Typeset in Adobe Caslon Pro
Printed on 80gsm Local Offset Paper

Printed by Kagzi Printers, Karachi

Contents

PART 3. DRAWING CONCLUSIONS

Acknowledgements

The authors are highly indebted to many individuals in the preparation of this book.

The original concept of the study was brainstormed with Johannes Linn, Ijaz Nabi, and Anil Sood, whose intellectual guidance served as a good starting point.

The detailed case studies, which are the underpinnings of the book, are the result of information, insights, opinions, meetings' facilitation, and logistical support of numerous individuals. Our special thanks go to: Naveed Ahmed, Imran Anwar, Ali Cheema, Javed Hamid, Zia ul Hasan, Ishrat Husain, Mohammad Ikram, Roqiya Bano Javed, Naila Khan, Noor Rehman Khan, Naim Mutaza, Rizwan Naseer, Anjum Nasim, Ijaz Nabi, Shams Bin Niazi, Mohammad Nishat, Mohammad Tahir Noor, Zafar Iqbal Qureshi, Naveed Jan Sahibzada, Faisal Sultan, Sibghat Ullah, Arif Zulficar, Ahmed Zaheer, Aneela Salman, and Naiman Jalil.

The work of the authors was ably supported by a team of competent research assistants who provided invaluable support throughout the preparation of this book. The team included: Haider Abbas, Khadija Anjum, Ali Hassan Ayub, Mah Afroze Chughtai, Amen Jalal, Tehmina Khan, Hira Mumtaz, Attiq ur Rehman and Osman Sajid.

Introduction

The purpose of this study is to explain how some entities can survive and flourish in an institutional environment that is both fragile and hostile. Despite daunting odds, some institutions have managed to succeed and effectively deliver core services, earn legitimacy in the eyes of the citizenry, and forge resilience in the face of an otherwise tumultuous and prohibitive operational context. Levy (2014) refers to these institutions as 'islands of effectiveness within a broader sea of institutional dysfunction'. A review of some case studies demonstrates that it is possible for a society, such as Pakistan's, to have effective organizations even in the face of a dismal overall picture.

White (1958) noted that even in the most corruption-ridden periods of nineteenth-century United States, there were some agencies that achieved and maintained high professional standards. Fischer and Lundgren (1975) observed that Britain possessed an extremely professional navy for well over a century, before it managed to reform its patronage-ridden and incompetent army. Daland (1981) observed that during Brazil's military dictatorships, some industrial enterprises were models of productivity, even while social service agencies were falling apart.

The question, therefore, is not whether successful agencies can exist in problematic environments, but what conditions make that possible.

First, however, we need to explain what we mean by success—what is it that differentiates these entities from their failing or average counterparts in a country.

We define success along three dimensions:[1]

1. **Results**: The selected institutions demonstrate sustained success in achieving their key objectives and outputs/outcomes. They have already achieved appreciable, measurable, and gradually improving results in terms of a significant portion of their mandates. The objective is not to establish a 'universal bar' for success across all cases, rather, it is to measure each entity's progress against the criteria for success it has defined for itself through interaction with stakeholders.

2. **Legitimacy**: Here the objective is to assess how clients perceive the agency and its functions as a whole, and their level of trust in how the institution exercises the authority entrusted to it. In assessing legitimacy, we focus on both output legitimacy (*what* the institution does, or its outward performance and the perceived quality of services delivered) as well as procedural legitimacy (*how* the institution functions, or the quality of its operational procedures that enable it to achieve success).[2]

3. **Sustainability/Resilience**: An institution that is durable and resilient can sustain and improve results over time and can adapt to changing circumstances, can anticipate new challenges, and can cope with exogenous shocks. For an institution to be considered durable and resilient, it should have maintained its performance through at least one transition in agency leadership or five years of successful operation (Barma 2013). Also, if the institution was established or initially maintained by external support (funding and/or technical assistance), it will have moved over time towards less reliance on external support and more on predictable (budgeted) stream of in-country resources for its continuing operations.

Clearly, these measures of success are closely interlinked. An entity's legitimacy depends, at least partially, on results and the achievement of its key objectives. Similarly, an institution that is considered legitimate is more likely to be resilient; in turn a more resilient institution has a greater opportunity to earn legitimacy and achieve results.

The study's research results are based mostly on semi-structured interviews with members of the selected institutions, including leaders, staff, and clients. A standard questionnaire was used for the interviews. In addition to the interviews, and where possible, a qualitative assessment was made of how the organizations are perceived as performing by the key stakeholders and general public.

Nine Pakistani institutions, in both the public and private sectors, generally regarded as successful, have been selected for the purpose of this research. These are: Lahore University of Management Sciences (LUMS); Institute of Business Administration (IBA); Motorway Police; Benazir Income Support Programme (BISP); National Database and Registration Authority (NADRA); Punjab Education Foundation (PEF); Edhi Foundation; Shaukat Khanum Memorial Cancer Hospital (SKMCH); and Rescue 1122. Major factors, internal as well as external that led to their success, have been examined. The private sector organizations selected for the study are those which operate in the social sector and are not-for-profit.

To make the analysis more meaningful, failing organizations are also examined, to assess why these organisations have failed. Two examples of such organizations included are Pakistan International Airlines (PIA) and Pakistan Railways (PR).

Chapter one assesses the various aspects of Pakistan's governance and institutional development and compares them with selected Asian countries. Chapter two reviews the literature on the subject and summarizes the determinants of success in general. This is followed by details on each of the nine successful enterprises in chapters three to eleven, and of the failing institutions in chapter twelve. Chapter thirteen, which is the main section of the study, gathers together the factors behind the success of the selected agencies, and chapter fourteen summarizes what remains to be done to enhance their performance further.

Finally, chapter fifteen pulls together the main conclusions of the study, draws some lessons for policymakers in dealing with the public organizations, and suggests areas of further research on this topic.

While significant literature exists that defines and measures public sector's institutional capacity,[3] much less attention has been given to defining the 'granular ingredients' of institutional success.[4] This study seeks to understand the factors behind the success of organizations in the institutionally challenged context of Pakistan. This decision to focus on successful entities is guided by the work of reputable authors: David Leonard (2010) points out a small but influential group of scholars—including himself, Norman Uphoff, Judith Tendler, and Samuel Paul—who have focused on successful institutions on the premise that 'it is dangerous to derive development prescriptions only from data that are largely dominated by failure'.

It is hoped that the research will have several audiences. One audience will be the federal and provincial governments and their international development partners. Another set would be the institutions themselves and also other institutions that aspire to better performance. Last, but not the least, the study will be of interest to academia to better understand the causal factors describing the success of these institutions.

1

Weak Institutional Environment

There is broad consensus that the pace and quality of economic and social development in a country is largely dependent on the quality of governance and institutions. Regardless of how sound economic policies are, the benefits of growth will be stymied unless the institutions underpinning these policies are viable, efficient, and effective.

Pakistan's main problem in sustaining macroeconomic stability, and delivering public services to the poor, is weak governance and a gradual but perceptible decline in institutional capacity (Husain 2012). This reflects the elitist nature of the state and society and the simultaneous conflict and collusion among the various power structures in the country. The situation is aggravated further by a lack of capacity to implement policies. Implementation capacity is in turn a function of the objectives of the political leadership, the competence of the civil service, and the strength of public institutions.

To be sure, there has been some progress during the last decade in selected areas of institution building. Since 2008, the judiciary has assumed significant power to check the arbitrariness of various state actions. This exercise of judicial review has increased to a point that judges of the Supreme Court have occasionally been criticized for being excessively interventionist and going beyond their jurisdictional domain. The legislature, despite its delays in lawmaking and excessive polarization, was able to pass overwhelmingly important legislation, such as the Eighteenth Amendment, which transfers power from the president to the prime minister and the legislature. The Amendment has also led to important delegation of power to the provincial governments, while strengthening the role of the Council on Common Interest, a joint federal-provincial forum. The previous Pakistan Peoples Party coalition government was able to survive its full term of five years, with an unprecedented transfer of power in May 2013, from one democratically-elected government to another. This change took place on the basis of elections that were considered generally free and fair by outside observers and were marked by a high turnout despite terrorists' threats to subvert them. The demonstrations and sit-ins (dharnas) during the latter part of 2014, against the alleged unfairness of the electoral outcome by two political parties, Pakistan Tehreek-i-Insaf (PTI) and Pakistan Awami Tehreek (PAT) remained remarkably peaceful and within constitutional parameters. In any case, in July 2015, a judicial commission rejected accusations of fraud and irregularities in the 2013 elections. Also, unlike in the past, the army did not intervene through a coup on grounds of political instability.

The Pakistani media has also, since 2002, become powerful, independent, and vibrant, with the number of private television channels burgeoning from just three state-run channels in 2000 to eighty-nine in 2012.[1] Although, sometimes criticized for being unprofessional, excessively sensationalist, and politically biased, these television channels have made a great contribution to raising the concerns of the common man and woman in urban and rural areas alike. The military continues to remain the strongest, best organized, and nationally most popular institution. Despite the slight dip in the image of the military in the aftermath of the US raid in May 2011 that killed Osama Bin Laden, some 80 per cent of Pakistanis still expressed confidence in the military.[2] During the past few years, the military has refrained from meddling in most political matters. This has brought a sense of stability to democratic governance in Pakistan.

However, as will become clear from this chapter, the problem is that these recent positive developments have not yet filtered down to result in tangible achievements. The purpose of this chapter is to assess the various aspects of Pakistan's institutional development and to compare them with selected Asian countries.

The institutional environment in a country is determined by the legal and administrative framework within which individuals, companies, and the government, interact to generate income and wealth. The quality of institutions has a strong impact on competitiveness and growth. Apart from influencing investment decisions and the organization of production, the quality of institutions plays an important role in ways in which a society distributes benefits and bears the costs of development strategies and policies.

There is more to the role of institutions than just the legal framework. The attitudes of government towards markets and efficiency of operations are also very important. Excessive bureaucracy and red tape, excessive regulation, corruption, lack of transparency, inability to provide appropriate services to the business sector, and political dependence of the judicial system, can impose large economic costs on businesses and can slow economic development.

While economic literature has typically focused on public institutions, the role of private institutions in economic development cannot be ignored. To avoid corporate scandals, the relevance of accounting and reporting standards and transparency for preventing fraud and mismanagement, ensuring good governance, and maintaining investor and consumer confidence, are also very important. Private sector transparency is indispensable to business and can be brought about through the use of standards as well as auditing and accounting practices that ensure access to information in a timely manner.

Based on these considerations and employing the World Economic Forum's Executive Opinion Survey for 2014–2015, Table 1.1 summarizes the rankings and scores on the overall quality of institutions for selected Asian countries, including Pakistan. As can be seen, Pakistan fares poorly (ranking 129 out of 144 countries) and the worst among the countries selected for comparison in these tables.

The data from the Executive Opinion Survey allows us to drill deeper into the various components of institutional development. For example, Table 1.2 provides rankings of countries for (a) diversion of public funds to companies and individuals due to corruption, (b) the level of public trust in

Table 1.1: Ranking of Overall Quality of Institutions, 2014–15

	Rank	Score
Bangladesh	109	3.7
India	71	4.2
Nepal	102	3.8
Pakistan	129	3.4
Sri Lanka	73	4.3
China	28	4.9
South Korea	26	5.0

Note: Ranks out of 144 countries and scores measured on a scale of 1 to 7.
Source: Adapted from World Economic Forum: Executive Opinion Survey, 2014–15.

politicians, (c) irregular payments and bribes, (d) favouritism in decisions of government officials, and (e) transparency of government policymaking. As the table indicates, taking the average of the above five indicators, Pakistan fares better than only Bangladesh. All the other countries in the selected sample (India, Sri Lanka, China, Nepal, and South Korea) have better or significantly better rankings.

Table 1.2: Various Indicators of Corruption
(rankings out of 144 countries), 2014–15

	Bangla-desh	India	Nepal	Pakistan	Sri Lanka	China	S. Korea
Diversion of funds due to corruption	106	60	92	94	85	45	67
Level of public trust in politicians	136	50	122	108	85	26	97
Irregular payments and bribes	140	93	119	123	91	66	52
Favouritism in government officials' decisions	131	49	91	101	98	22	82
Transparency of government policymaking	114	64	117	118	88	33	133
Average of above[a]	125	63	108	109	89	38	86

[a]: Simple arithmetic average of the five categories.

Source: Adapted from World Economic Forum: Executive Opinion Survey, 2014–15.

Table 1.3 summarizes survey results for two categories of questions: (i) how burdensome is it for businessmen in the country to comply with governmental administrative requirements? And (ii) how efficient is the legal framework in the country for private businesses in settling disputes? The table demonstrates that India, China, South Korea, and Sri Lanka, perform better than Pakistan, while Bangladesh and Nepal perform worse.

Table 1.3: Regulatory and Judicial Efficiency (rankings out of 144 countries), 2014–15

	Bangla-desh	India	Nepal	Pakistan	Sri Lanka	China	S. Korea
Burden of government regulation	109	59	106	103	91	19	96
Legal efficiency in settling disputes	123	57	120	101	28	49	82
Average of above[a]	116	58	113	102	59	34	89

[a]: Simple arithmetic average of the two categories.

Source: Adapted from World Economic Forum: Executive Opinion Survey, 2014–15.

Another important set of questions is the degree to which terrorism, crime and violence, and organized crime, impose costs on businesses in the country, and the reliability of police services in the country.

Table 1.4 provides the rankings for this set of categories. It indicates the rather intuitive conclusion that Pakistan is worse off in the rankings compared to the other six Asian countries, and its ranking on the business costs of terrorism is amongst the worst in all 144 countries for which data is available. This is clearly a reflection of the current terrorism, other crime, and violence, including organized crime, in Pakistan, especially in Karachi, the hub of Pakistan's business activities. The table also indicates that the reliability of the Pakistani police, in enforcing law and order is better only than Bangladesh, among the other six Asian countries.

Table 1.5 summarizes the performance of other selected aspects of institutional development and governance in Pakistan and these six Asian countries. The two categories are:

- The protection of property rights, including financial assets.
- The independence of the judiciary from influences of members of government, citizens, or firms.

Table 1.4: Security Problems and Reliability of Police Services (rankings out of 144 countries), 2014–15

	Bangla-desh	India	Nepal	Pakistan	Sri Lanka	China	S. Korea
Business costs of terrorism	114	125	119	139	17	85	115
Business costs of crime & violence	116	98	119	132	54	52	76
Business costs of organized crime	97	114	129	137	67	70	93
Reliability of police services	138	88	87	127	100	62	48
Average of above[a]	116	106	113	134	59	67	83

[a]: Simple arithmetic average of the four categories.

Source: Adapted from World Economic Forum: Executive Opinion Survey, 2014–15.

In the case of judicial independence, Pakistan ranks behind only India and China, but the ranking for the protection of property rights is better only than Bangladesh.

Table 1.5: Performance in other Selected Institutional Aspects (rankings out of 144 countries), 2014–15

	Bangla-desh	India	Nepal	Pakistan	Sri Lanka	China	S. Korea
Protection of property rights	123	73	119	121	57	50	64
Judicial independence	132	50	92	67	72	60	82
Average of above[a]	127	61	105	94	64	55	73

[a]: Simple arithmetic average of the three categories.
Source: Adapted from World Economic Forum: Executive Opinion Survey, 2014–15.

Finally, as indicated earlier, the role of private institutions in the economy is an important aspect of institutional development. In this set of categories, the questions that arise are: What are the corporate ethics of firms in the country? What is the strength of auditing and reporting standards? What is the efficacy in corporate governance of investors and boards of directors in the country?

Table 1.6 once again illustrates that, in these categories, Pakistan averages below India, Sri Lanka, China, and South Korea, ahead only of Bangladesh and Nepal.

In short, in almost all aspects of governance and institutional development summarized above, Pakistan trails behind the four countries in the sample, namely India, Sri Lanka, China, and South Korea. It only fares favourably compared to Bangladesh and Nepal.

Acemoglu and Robinson (2012), in their remarkably compelling book, try to address the question that has baffled economists and sociologists for a long time: Why is it that some countries are rich and others poor, divided by wealth and poverty, education and literacy, health and sickness, and abundance and famine?[3] After disqualifying a number of commonly-expounded theories that attempt to answer the question with theories about geography, genetics, and culture, the authors argue that the best explanation of the distribution of wealth in the world is institutional.

Table 1.6: Selected Indicators of Private Institution, 2014–15

	Bangla-desh	India	Nepal	Pakistan	Sri Lanka	China	S. Korea
Ethical behaviour of firms	140	88	128	111	82	55	95
Strength of auditing and reporting standards	133	102	121	90	55	82	84
Efficacy of corporate boards	132	94	115	119	33	78	126
Average of above[a]	135	95	121	107	57	72	102

[a]: Simple arithmetic average of the three categories.

Source: Adapted from World Economic Forum: Executive Opinion Survey, 2014–15.

In particular, the authors argue that rich countries are rich because they have 'inclusive institutions', that is to say, economic and political institutions that include the large majority of the population in the political and economic community. Inclusive institutions tend to be democratic, allowing masses to vote and protect free speech in a manner that enables institutions to respond to the interests of all citizens. Inclusive institutions also set out clear property rights that are reliably enforced and have sufficient central authority to be able to provide basic social services such as education, health, water and sanitation, and social safety nets.

This, according to the authors, explains why Botswana has become one of the fastest growing countries in the world, while other African nations such as Zimbabwe and Sierra Leone are mired in poverty and violence. This also explains why, despite the homogeneity of their population, North Korea is among the poorest countries in the world while their counterparts in South Korea are among the richest. The South was able to forge a society that created incentives, rewarded innovation, and allowed everyone to avail economic opportunities. The resulting economic success was sustained because the government became accountable and responsive to citizens. By contrast, the people of the North endured decades of political oppression and famine, and very different institutions which essentially remain extractive and absolutist.

Effective institutions and good governance, together with well-designed policies and their implementation, are the essential elements for sustained and equitable growth (Husain 1999). Good governance incorporates a system of checks and balances in a country's institutional infrastructure, enabling politicians and bureaucrats to pursue the common good, while restraining arbitrary action and corruption. The state's monopoly on both coercion and access to information gives rise to opportunities for public officials to promote their own interests or those of their friends at the expense of those of the citizenry. Under these circumstances, there is a high probability for rent-seeking and corruption.

The above is a good explanation for the reasons behind the dismal state of Pakistan's economic and social situation. Over the span of sixty-eight years of Pakistan's independence, the country has been subjected to strict military rule for almost thirty years. To a large extent, this has prevented the development of more inclusive institutions. At the same time, civil society organizations, which typically serve to respond to the social, economic, and humanitarian needs of the society at a grassroots level, have been discouraged and generally viewed with suspicion. Corruption has become rampant and successive governments—civilian or military—have failed to address the needs of the citizenry.

Thus, a question often raised in Pakistan and elsewhere: Why is it that Pakistani professionals (doctors, lawyers, economists, etc.) excel abroad, but are unable to do a decent job in their own country? The answer clearly lies in the weak and corrupt institutions of the country that sap the enthusiasm and dedication of its professionals.

In many developed countries such as Italy, governments change with great frequency, but this has little impact on their economy or social development because in these countries institutions work. In Pakistan, and in other countries with fragile institutions, every political development sends disturbing reverberations through the system. Since priorities are not driven by the citizens' needs, the focus changes to distractions. As Khan (2012) notes: 'As a form of political gimmickry, we are made to believe that creating new provinces shall solve all the problems of the poor. They shall inherit the same *thanedar* and *patwari*'.[4]

Institutional strengthening requires long-term commitment, which successive governments in Pakistan—civilian or military—have failed to provide. Elected governments, with their focus on the next elections, and military governments desperate to gain legitimacy, get mired in ad hoc and occasionally populist measures without addressing the key objectives of building institutional capacity, and setting up a viable governance structure (Husain 2012).

In short, Pakistan suffers from a weak institutional set-up, which is not just shaky but also deteriorating over time. Good governance, macroeconomic stability, and the delivery of critically-important social services to the citizenry, cannot progress without a determined effort to build viable institutions. The purpose here is not to discuss needed actions, but to highlight the urgency of the matter. A summary of the requisite measures is provided in other sources (see for example, Husain 2012).

In the following chapters, several successful Pakistani entities are examined, which seem to perform well and flourish in this relatively inhospitable institutional environment. The factors behind their success are summarized. At the same time, the causes behind two failing organizations are enumerated for comparative purposes. It is hoped that the results of this study will be of interest to policymakers and academics alike.

2

General Determinants of Success

Introduction

In the previous chapter, we summarized the evidence of Pakistan's weak institutional and governance structure. It was demonstrated that, even by comparison with South Asian neighbours, Pakistan has a fragile institutional set up and governance, aggravated further by the ongoing militancy and organized crime in urban areas, especially Karachi. Elitist barriers and complacent governments have inhibited inclusive growth, reflected, for example, in the dismal state of education in the country. The entrepreneurial spirit of the citizens (who excel abroad in all fields) is stifled by the weak and corrupt institutions of the country.

The main purpose of the remaining chapters of this study is to understand how and why some Pakistani organizations are performing well despite the hostile and fragile milieu within which they operate. How is it that some of them excel in the achievement of their goals not only domestically but also on the international arena? What are the underpinnings of success for these institutions? Are the factors specific to the institutions or are they generalizable?

Before we examine the success factors, we need to answer at least three relevant questions. First, what do we mean by 'success'? Second, why have we selected the nine successful institutions mentioned in the introductory chapter? And third, what do we mean by 'institutions' in the context of this study?

The definition of 'success' has already been articulated in the introductory chapter. Success in our context is defined in terms of three intertwining dimensions. An institution— public or private—should demonstrate *sustained and measurable success* in attaining its key objectives and outputs/outcomes. An institution should gain *legitimacy* with its clients by winning their trust in how it utilizes the authority entrusted to it. And an institution should *be durable and resilient* enough to adapt successfully to changing circumstances and to cope with unpleasant exogenous shocks.

In terms of the logic behind the selection of the nine institutions in this study, clearly there are many other successful entities in Pakistan, as can be expected in a country with a population of over 180 million. The scope of the work, however, was such that we had to limit the number to less than ten. That said, all efforts were made to compile as diverse a sample as possible. So, for example, we have included in the sample two educational institutions of higher learning (one private, one public), a provincial education foundation that is public, but enjoys a substantial degree of managerial autonomy, a motorway police organization, two emergency response institutions (one private, one public), a not-for-profit hospital, a public agency that runs and maintains government databases and statistically manages the sensitive registration of databases of all Pakistanis and Pakistani-origin individuals, and a public organization that serves as a social safety net for the neediest citizens of the country. In this way, there is adequate coverage not only with regard to the public/private classification but also in terms of sectors covered. To complement the analysis, a review is also carried out of two failing organizations to understand the reasons for their failure.

Finally, what do we mean by 'institutions' as used in this study? We do not use the term in the new institutional economics definition of institutions (see North 1990) as 'rules of the game' or established social practices. These rules of the game include formal systems such as the constitution, laws, taxation, insurance, and market regulations. They also include informal norms of behaviour, such as habits, customs, and ideologies. A society's economic well-being is determined by the extent to which these formal and informal systems exist. By contrast, we use the term in its more colloquial meaning, that is, interchangeably with 'entity,' 'agency,' or 'organization'. Our objective is to examine these organizations in a weak, corruption-ridden, non-inclusive and/or absolutist institutional environment.

LITERATURE REVIEW ON THE INGREDIENTS OF INSTITUTIONAL SUCCESS

Examining the factors behind the success of firms is nothing new. One of the earliest investigations was undertaken by

Peters and Waterman (1982), who concluded that there are eight common features of the chosen corporations that made them successful:

- A bias for proactivity, active decision-making—'getting on with it'. The leaders of these firms facilitate quick decision-making and problem-solving, cutting through red tape.
- Close to the customer—learning from their clients.
- Autonomy and entrepreneurship—fostering innovation and nurturing potential 'champions'.
- Productivity through people—prioritizing the development of employees as a high priority.
- Hands-on value-driven management philosophy.
- 'Stick to the knitting'—stay with the business that you know and not overstretch into areas where the company may not have a competitive advantage.
- Lean staff and especially minimal staff at headquarters.
- Simultaneous loose-tight properties—autonomy in shop floor combined with centralized control.

With the benefit of hindsight, several of the corporations that Peters and Waterman selected as success stories did not perform well at all during the 1980s, such as NCR, Wang, Xerox, and others. However, the book spawned a series of publications that tried to address the success factors behind the performance of corporations. Key (1995) argued that there is excessive importance given to size and scale and to leadership vision as a determinant of corporate success. He asserted that competitive advantage and corporate success are generally based on stability, continuity in relationships, and on the identification and exploitation of specific capabilities. The case for the latter is made through the contrast of three stories of business success (BMW, Glaxo, and Honda) and three stories of business failures (Saatchi & Saatchi, Groupe Bull, and EMI). Key argued that the three successful companies were able to identify their 'distinctive capabilities', select the markets best suited to their strengths, and build effective competitive strategies to exploit them. By contrast, the three failing firms were characterized by the inability to match the capabilities to their aspirations (Bull), a misreading of their own competitive strengths (Saatchi & Saatchi), and misreading of its relationships with competitors and customers despite their distinctive capabilities (EMI).

In a follow-up book, Key (1995) applies economic theories to guide managers in creating successful corporate strategies. The author argues that firms have unique strengths that they must comprehend and utilize. These strengths are in four general areas: (i) their reputation; (ii) how well they create innovative new products or services; (iii) special strategic assets or market positions they may have; and (iv) how they are organized and how they operate. A different, institutional approach to the success of firms is adopted by Munir and Phillips (2005), who examine the role played by entrepreneurs in bringing about institutional change in the adoption of a radically new technology. Specifically, they examine how Kodak was able to have a breakthrough in sales by transforming photography from a highly-specialized activity for professional photographers to one that became an everyday activity.

In *Good to Great* (Collins 2001), a study of how some private sector firms had transformed themselves from good companies to great companies, factors such as leadership, hiring, and maintaining the right staff, a strong belief in the organization's goals, a culture of discipline, and the use of technology to accelerate improvements are cited as factors for success.

Roberts (2007) argues that there are predictable and necessary relationships among changes in firms relating to organizational designs, formal architecture, policies and processes, and their corporate culture that will determine their growth and performance. Organizations that are successful establish 'patterns of fit' among the various elements of their organizational designs, their competitive strategies, and the external environment in which they operate, and they do so in a holistic manner. He focuses the discussion on such topics as a firm's unique capabilities, its culture, and its architecture.

Turning to the performance of public organizations, the World Bank (1995) report argued that 'bureaucrats typically perform poorly in business not because they are incompetent (they are not) but because they face contradictory goals and perverse incentives that can distract and discourage even very able and dedicated public servants'. The issue is not the people in the system but the circumstances in which they find themselves as bureaucrats in business. The book examines the high cost of running state-owned enterprises, which siphon off needed resources from basic social services.

Shleifer (1998) also addresses the issue of ownership as the key determinant of performance. He argues that private ownership should generally be preferred to public ownership when the incentives to innovate and to contain costs are strong. Also, many of the concerns that private firms fail to address 'social goals' can be addressed through government contracting and regulation, without resort to government ownership.

In an earlier book, Ayub and Hegstad (1986) had tackled the issue of factors behind the success of public industrial enterprises more directly. According to the authors, leaving aside the issue of ownership, there are three main explanatory factors behind the success of state-owned companies: (i) how competitive the environment is within which the enterprise operates—state enterprises subject to a more demanding, competitive environment tend to perform better; (ii) the greater the financial autonomy and accountability of the enterprise, the greater the incentive for better performance; and (iii) the extent and manner in which managerial autonomy and accountability are ensured also has an impact on performance.

Moving more closely to the subject of this book, academics and policymakers concur that there are both internal and external dimensions that explain the success of organizations in hostile environments and that these two dimensions are interrelated and interactive. Leonard (2010) focuses on 'pockets' of institutional effectiveness in countries with poor governance and weak institutional set-up. In reviewing the literature on this subject, he generates five 'meta-hypotheses'—two of which are internal and three external—and examines how they interact. Grosh (1991), Tendler (1997), and Owuso (2006), have all explored the existence of successful public organizations in the midst of prevailing poor governance. Grindle (1997) enumerates four features of relatively successful entities in otherwise unfavourable developing country contexts, stating that successful organizations:

- develop an organizational 'mystique' or an internalized sense of mission and success; have proactive, problem-solving, and team-oriented managers who are seen as equitable and flexible;
- have well-defined performance standards and expectations;
- have sufficient autonomy in personnel management.

Israel (1987) focuses on how an agency's performance is to some extent determined by the degree to which its functions are 'specific', i.e. are highly technical and specialized (for example a central bank compared to a ministry of education). More recently, Fukuyama (2004) has also used the concept of specificity to suggest that the success of institutional reform efforts is more assured in agencies where tasks are highly specific and the volume of transactions is low because these are the entities in which monitoring outputs and accountability are most likely.

Setting aside the internal workings of an organization and moving to the external environment it confronts, and within which it has to exist, there is general agreement that institutions have a higher probability of success in demanding contexts when they are able to 'identify, tap into, and build on pre-existing capacity—whether this capacity is situated within the agency, in other public institutions, or non-governmental or civic groups' (Barma 2013). The key to using existing capacity is to better align the administrative and financial strategies of the agency with the broader public financial management and human resource systems in the country (Cliffe and Manning 2008) or, at a minimum, devise creative ways of circumventing the constraints imposed on the agency by the macro-system.

Manor (2007) argues, based on detailed empirical case studies that entities which challenge institutional environments are more likely to succeed if they design and implement programmes in close consultation with local stakeholders. The extent to which an institution is able to maintain a successful client orientation and to achieve its objectives is determined by the extent and manner in which it collaborates with other partners, such as civil society organizations, public agencies, and the private sector.

The main proposition of Abah (2012) is that in dysfunctional environments, the most critical ingredient for attaining and sustaining good public sector performance is demand. He argues that, while all other causal factors such as management and leadership are important, demand sits on top of the hierarchy. Reformers should, therefore, focus on creating or aligning with the demand for improvement. The demand for improved performance could emanate from the government, the private sector, donors, pressure groups, and beneficiaries of services. The existence of demand catalyses good performance; where it exists, it will create the environment for the other causal factors to come into play. Abah bases his work on pairing similar organizations in the same sectors in Nigeria—one successful and the other not—and tries to extract the explanatory factors for success.

In a recent book, Levy (2014) recommends an approach of working 'with the grain,' under which reform is perceived as evolutionary, being characterized as 'good fit' rather than 'first best' or optimal. This approach states that reforms cannot be re-engineered from scratch but need to be aligned with local institutional realities. The aim is to push things along, striving for gains that initially may seem modest, but can give rise to 'a cascading sequence of change for the better'.

GENERAL DETERMINANTS OF SUCCESS

Drawing from the literature on the underpinnings of success among public and private not-for-profit entities, we can highlight the key factors of success along two dimensions—internal and external.[1] These are general factors applicable to most entities of the type indicated. Successful organizations in countries with fragile institutions appear to share a series of attributes in their internal management that enable them to achieve good results and improved efficiency. The following is a list—by no means exhaustive—of these internal dimension factors.

1. **Well-defined mission which is translated into outcomes and results:** Successful organizations typically have developed a mission that is easily identified by staff at all levels and by relevant stakeholders. Moreover, the mission can be translated into defined outcomes and results. There are no extraneous objectives that would detract from the core mission, and there are no pressures from outside (mainly government) to undertake activities that are not central to the organization's mission.

2. **Attracting and deploying skilled staff:** A critically important factor behind the success of organizations is their ability to attract competent staff, retain them for continuity, and invest in their skill development. These institutions have been able to mobilize and build on existing skills, competitively recruit senior and middle management, train new employees, and retain them over the medium and long-term. The organizations have developed new processes to motivate people to improve their performance, together with restructuring of work processes to better meet the organizations' key objectives. Performance evaluation links the achievement of certain goals to rewards (cash payments and in-kind) and career advancement opportunities. Access to training and international exposure is an important magnet in attracting candidates. The ability to attract

and retain staff is also a function of remuneration and benefits.

3. **Continuity of leadership and management:** An important success factor is continuity of tenure of top leadership and senior management. There is nothing more disruptive to the work of an institution than high turnover of its management and staff, resulting in lost human capital. Success of institutions depends on long-term commitment of leaders and public entrepreneurs. It takes at least a decade to get real traction for certain important items on the agenda of organizational leaders: to define clear and implementable sets of tasks, to develop internal capabilities and external alliances, and to pursue implementation to a point of sufficient critical mass to prevent reversal of progress once the leaders/ champions move from their positions. Over time, institutions can strengthen incrementally, gradually transforming personalized leadership into more impersonal institutionally based leadership. However, in the interim, the role of public entrepreneurs and leaders is indispensable. Stability of a core group of managers and senior staff is crucial in maintaining an organization's institutional memory and the ability to operate effectively in an often tumultuous institutional environment. Longer tenure of senior and middle management also contributes to improved implementation of projects and programmes and

allows for more continuous leadership and greater accountability.

4. **Financial autonomy:** To a large extent, an institution's managerial autonomy is determined by the degree to which it is dependent on state or outside funds for its operations. Agencies that are not heavily dependent on outside financial resources typically have more say in their day-to-day work and management. A successful organization has a substantial portion of its expenditures covered from its own resources so that it is not subject to fluctuations in state funds allocated to it.

5. **Good internal communications and employee participation:** Successful organizations hold regular meetings at various levels and have good information-sharing mechanisms. To improve performance as a result of information sharing and employee participation, these organizations hold consultations and regular communications with staff. This type of internal communication helps improve the morale of the staff, enhances their understanding of programmes, and gives them the opportunity to voice their concerns to senior management.

6. **Strong and visionary leadership:** In many cases, successful organizations are blessed with visionary leaders who are fully committed to the success of the organization and command respect with all key stakeholders. Given their strong leadership, they

play a strong advocacy role as well as in mobilizing financial resources for the entity. They are well connected with the key actors in the society and are able to navigate through troubled waters of the bureaucracy. The leadership should not overtly engage in party politics but should be sufficiently politically savvy to defend the organization's interests. It is difficult to overestimate the importance of these leaders to the success of their organizations.

7. **Building learning organizations:** A characteristic of successful organizations is that they encourage employees to innovate and to take risks to better perform their duties. These organizations also provide staff the necessary training and the right tools for greater efficiency. They also have mechanisms in place to incorporate ongoing learning through periodic reviews and needed adjustments as well as through curtailing activities that fail to achieve intended outcomes. Giving employees opportunities for participation, learning, and self-development improves employee morale and motivation.

8. **Results-oriented organizational culture and cohesive identity:** In successful organizations, employees typically share values, beliefs, norms of appropriate behaviour, specialized language, and symbols. These components of culture tell employees how to perceive, think about, and feel about something, and what to pay attention to. Organizational culture is typically expressed in

symbols, logos, rituals, and ceremonies. Leaders in such organizations have developed formal statements of their organization's philosophy and employed stories about events and people to reinforce key messages about the history and aspirations of the organization. Organizational success is celebrated as a collective achievement, which reinforces the strong identification of staff with their organization.

In addition to the above internal factors that underpin success, there are other factors related to how an organization copes with its *external* environment: its stakeholders, clients, and financiers. Some of these factors are summarized below.

9. **Ability to cope with political pressures**: Institutions that are able to avoid pressure on their management to circumvent their processes and procedures (such as pressures to ignore established selection criteria) are more successful. Leadership of the institutions plays an important buffering role in this process. There are some institutions that manage to withstand pressures by staying under the 'political radar' and building their own coalition of support as they pursue their respective mandates.

10. **Displaying results to mobilize support**: A common feature of successful institutions is that they have managed to mobilize resources to fund their mandates. The ability to demonstrate effectiveness, report results, and obtain external recognition, has

been critical to the mobilization of resources. These organizations use their basic monitoring and data collection systems to document their activities and achievements and show decision-makers that the financial resources are being used well.

11. **Role of development partners**: Some institutions, either through strong efforts or through good luck, have benefited from outside support at critical points in their development. For example, institutions have received external funding to finance needed infrastructure, which has facilitated the operations of the institution. Again, in these cases, leadership of the institutions has played a catalytic role in attracting funding through demonstration of a good track record and achievement of stated objectives.

In the next nine chapters, we examine the nine institutions that meet some or most of the criteria of success outlined earlier. We specifically summarize the success factors of each institution, analysing why these institutions are successful and what the remaining issues and challenges are that would need to be addressed to enhance their performance further. Following the chapters on successful organizations, we include a chapter on two failing institutions and summarize the reasons for their failure. Finally, in the last three chapters, we pull together all the common factors of success and draw broad conclusions and lessons that can guide managers of similar institutions as well as policymakers and academics.

3

Lahore University of Management Sciences

INTRODUCTION

It is now well established and recognized that higher education plays an important, positive role not only in developed and middle-income economies, but also in low-income countries. By building a skilled, productive labour force and by adopting new ideas and technologies, higher education can enable these countries to become more globally competitive and successful on the international scene.

Among higher education institutions, what distinguishes the more successful and elite institutions from the rest are a number of basic features: highly-qualified faculty, excellence in teaching and learning, quality research, adequate funding from government and/or non-government sources, highly talented students, adequate academic freedom, well-defined autonomous governance structures, and well-equipped facilities for teaching, research, and administration (Niland 2007). It is the continuous and dynamic interaction among these features that separates the best universities from the rest.

In this chapter and the next, we examine two high-class Pakistani higher education institutions: one publicly owned (Institute of Business Administration, IBA) and the other a private one (Lahore Universityof Management Sciences, LUMS). The former was established almost sixty years ago in the formative years of the country itself, and went through its ups and downs. The latter is younger, slightly over 30 years old, and despite issues to be addressed, has managed to maintain a sustained record of excellence.

Different lessons emerge from the analysis of these two case studies. Among the factors that seem to be most relevant are leadership, financial sustainability, the ability to continually focus on a clear set of goals and institutional policies, development of a vibrant academic culture, and quality of the academic staff. An overarching factor and one that is critically important in the case of these two centres of learning, particularly in the case of IBA, is the unsettled political and security situation in the country. These two case studies illustrate that it is possible, against difficult challenges in Pakistan's weak institutional structure, to build successful learning institutions.

BACKGROUND ON LUMS

LUMS was established by sponsors belonging to the country's leading private and public sector corporations as the first private university in the country. The goal of the sponsors—led by the well-known businessman, Syed Babar Ali—was to establish a high quality business school comparable to leading business schools around the world.

It was also created with a view to provide a peaceful environment for the pursuit of learning at a time of disarray and strife in Pakistan's universities. Over time, the vision was expanded to transform the institution to a full-fledged university that would provide rigorous and broad-based academic and intellectual training.

LUMS was granted a charter by the government in March 1985. This charter gave the university the legal right to establish degree-granting programmes. Initial staffing was put in place, and Javed Hamid was named the first director. He brought a great deal of experience to the new institution and was responsible for adopting the Harvard Business School case method for LUMS' curriculum.

For several years, the MBA programme was the only programme at LUMS. Infrastructure, consisting of LUMS' rented facility in the Liberty area of Lahore, was inadequate. However, good standards were already established. The staff was relatively well-paid and the faculty recruited was of a high quality and disciplined. There was feedback on faculty teaching. A visiting committee was established with individuals from Harvard Business School, IMD Switzerland, Stockholm School of Economics, and the Asian Institute of Management Studies in the Philippines. This served as a performance audit.

During the fall of 1993, there was a shift to the new, 100-acre campus in Lahore's Defence Housing Authority, with USD10 million funding from USAID and its own matching funds. In 1994, the first BSc class for undergraduates was added, so the institution went beyond the business school. Currently, there are four schools; These are the Mushtaq Ahmad Gurmani School of Humanities and Social Sciences (MGSHSS); Syed Babar Ali School of Science and Engineering (SBASSE); Suleman Dawood School of Business (SDSB); and Shaikh Ahmad Hassan School of Law (SAHSOL). An Executive MBA programme was launched in 2002 to provide on-the-job training to managers and entrepreneurs. In addition, LUMS offers a wide array of executive courses and today is considered the finest institution in the country offering executive education.

From an initial thirty-nine students in the first class of 1986, the student body increased to about 3,200 in 2012–13. Similarly the faculty has increased from 7 to 164 (see Table 3.1).

The board of trustees—the policymaking body of the university—consists of leading members of the business community, academia, and representatives of the government. The principal functions of the board are to set broad policy guidelines and to review the operations of the university. The board of governors, who are also the sponsors of LUMS, raise the necessary funds for the university's operation and maintenance. The board of governors meets twice a year and the management committee, which consists of five or six members, meets every two weeks to address day-to-day issues. Many board members, as representatives of the business community, form a crucial link between the university and the business world. In terms of sources of income for operations and maintenance, the largest component comes from tuition fees (between 55 per cent and 70 per cent), followed by other income and receipts from the executive development programmes (Table 3.2).

Table 3.1: Growth in Full Time Students and Faculty

Year	Students	Faculty	Faculty: Student Ratio
1999–2000	680	44	1:15
2000–2001	848	44	1:19
2001–2002	1,058	53	1:20
2002–2003	1,276	68	1:19
2003–2004	1,650	85	1:19
2004–2005	2,111	100	1:21
2005–2006	1,704	104	1:16
2006–2007	1,765	117	1:15
2007–2008	1,731	115	1:15
2008–2009	1,840	123	1:15
2009–2010	2,037	136	1:15
2010–2011	2,574	151	1:17
2011–2012	2,587	149	1:17
2012–2013	3,238	164	1:20

Source: Various LUMS Annual Reports.

LUMS has a need-blind enrolment policy. It aims to provide equal academic opportunities to students of all social walks across Pakistan. To achieve this aim and to fully harness the potential of the human resources of the country, LUMS endeavours to provide a broader access to its programmes across the country.

Table 3.2: University's Operating Revenue (as % of total)

	FY 2000	FY 2006	FY 2012
Tuition Fees	54	62	69
Executive Development Programmes	15	10	8
Sponsored & Consultancy Projects	3	10	2
Other Income	22	16	20
Investment Income	6	2	1

Source: Various Annual Reports.

The National Outreach Programme (NOP) was launched in 2001 with the objective of providing educational opportunities to bright and talented students from smaller cities, villages, and inner-city areas of large urban centres unable to meet LUMS' regular fee requirements. Deserving students not well-prepared academically undergo 'remedial sessions' in areas such as English, mathematics, and interpersonal skills. As Table 3.3 indicates, NOP scholars have grown rapidly over the past decade.

REASONS FOR SUCCESS

LUMS has received accreditation of the South Asian Quality Assurance System (SAQS), one of only two Pakistani higher education institutions to do so (the other is the Institute of Business Administration, see Chapter four). Its graduates continue to be hired by top companies in the country and the region, as well as in academia and government. A large number of its graduates are admitted in the masters and doctoral programmes of reputed universities in North America, UK, and Australia. Graduates of LUMS

Table 3.3: Cumulative NOP Scholars

Year	Cumulative Numbers
2002	5
2003	14
2004	24
2005	34
2006	58
2007	110
2008	193
2009	330
2010	410
2011	464
2012	518

Source: LUMS Annual Reports.

hold jobs in many countries abroad (see Table 3.4). Its faculty is involved in providing consulting advice to the federal and local governments as well as to international donors.

What have been the factors that have enabled LUMS to become one of the top Pakistani and South Asian universities in a relatively short span of time since its foundation some thirty years ago?

As with most successful universities in the world, a key requisite is strong leadership that has a clear vision of the institution's mission and goals, and a clearly articulated process to translate the vision into concrete programmes and targets. It requires a leadership that has the ability to raise funding for the institution. And it needs a leadership that empowers faculty and staff to perform their functions within the framework established.

A critically important factor in the success of LUMS, particularly in its formative years, was the quality of its leadership. The Pro-Vice Chancellor of LUMS, Syed Babar Ali, is a successful corporate leader of the country and is internationally well known and well-respected. He perceived the need and the opportunity for an institution that would meet the industry's demand for good managers and leaders. His international stature was critically important; both for funding and attracting and retaining competent faculty, and for exposure of the faculty and students to the business community. Business leaders were invited to lecture, and field visits were arranged for students. Quality staff was selected so that even with just about a dozen faculty members at that time, the institution became recognized for excellence. All this would have been impossible without the leadership of Syed Babar Ali.

Syed Babar Ali was also a great delegator. While he kept himself well informed and focused on big picture matters, he left a great deal to the first director of LUMS, Javed Hamid, who had moved temporarily to LUMS from the International Finance Corporation of the World Bank Group.

Javed Hamid's experience at Harvard Business School led him to recommend the use of the case method of teaching, and Syed Babar Ali bought into the proposal. It is interesting that the design of the new campus and the method of teaching were dictated at least in part by the adoption of the case method.

Table 3.4: LUMS Alumni Employed by Country/Region

Country/Region	Number of alumni	Number of alumni employed
Pakistan	4,176	2,135
Middle East	338	310
United States	294	187
UK	120	103
East Asia	71	52
Canada	66	43
Continental Europe	56	43
South Asia	29	23
Africa	15	11
Other	5	3
Profile not updated	1, 893	44
Total	7, 063	2, 954

Including Australia.
Source: LUMS Annual Reports.

LUMS' leadership established early credibility with the government. For example, it did not request free land from the government for the construction of the new campus. Instead, the leadership requested help in facilitating the adoption of its charter, which was made easier.

A key factor was the early inculcation of the value system. The focus was strictly on merit-based selection of faculty and students. Students were selected through a rigorous process in which their academic potential, communications skills, intellectual prowess, leadership qualities, work stamina, and commitment to hard work were evaluated. This tradition has been maintained. For example, during the past decade, on average only 25 per cent of applicants for the BSc were selected (see Table 3.5).

Discipline was maintained, with everything being done on time. The resulting pressure of the workload on the students was seen as good training for them to operate successfully under deadline pressures. 'Even at the old, rented campus, when one entered the campus, one felt that one was in a completely different environment.' A long-term vision was established, 'not for a decade but for a century'[1]. Right from the beginning, the focus was on building an institution of excellence. Processes were put in place to help the realization of these goals.

Table 3.5: Undergraduate (BSc) Admissions

Year	Total no. of applicants	% admitted
2000	872	28
2001	996	32
2002	1,405	31
2003	1,691	30
2004	1,388	34
2005	2,264	24
2006	2,905	19
2007	1,795	28
2008	3,630	15
2009	3,538	35
2010	6,822	13
2011	5,402	17

Source: LUMS Annual Reports.

The faculty was young and energetic, some 78 per cent with doctoral degrees (see Table 3.6) and three to four years of experience. They were trained in the case method by visiting professors. There was feedback on teaching by foreign professors. Weekly meetings of the faculty were held to look ahead to upcoming lectures, and there was strong peer pressure on the faculty. Local case studies were gradually developed to make them more relevant to the country's context. At that time, the focus was almost entirely on teaching and little on research. Although some of the researchers felt frustrated, students were the beneficiaries.

Campus development leads to the foundation of a solid infrastructure base for adapting a university's strategic development goals, improving teaching and research quality, and meeting the expanding enrolment. LUMS was considerably helped by the building of its new, well-designed and well-equipped campus, with a USD10 million donation from USAID in 1988—its first involvement with a private institution in Pakistan. LUMS shifted to the new facility in 1993.

On the demand side, several factors were at play. There was a push from the business community of Pakistan for an institution that would serve their need for good managers and corporate leaders.

Table 3.6: Faculty Breakdown

Year	Faculty Number	PhD	non-PhD	% of Faculty with PhD
2000	38	31	7	81
2001	44	38	6	86
2002	54	47	7	87
2003	75	52	13	83
2004	87	na	87	-
2005	91	72	19	79
2006	104	83	21	80
2007	117	95	22	81
2008	115	78	37	68
2009	123	86	37	70
2010	136	90	46	66
2011	151	na	na	-
2012	149	na	na	-
2013	164	135	29	82

Source: LUMS.

Secondly, there was a lacuna to be filled. The public higher education system had essentially collapsed, and even the respected Institute of Business Administration (IBA) in Karachi was in the doldrums at that time (see Chapter four). This gave LUMS an opportunity to establish itself as a credible institution. Also on the demand side, there was a growing middle class in the country which could afford to pay LUMS' tuition fees for their children's education, but not the five to ten times higher tuition for education abroad.

Central to the success of a university is adequate and stable funding. Universities will be increasingly challenged to raise their own funds from potential donors, consulting, and from student tuition fees. In the case of LUMS, the core funding was provided by the initial five or six National Management Foundation donors. Syed Babar Ali was active in seeking foreign funding for the university from The Rausing Trust and USAID. Initially, 70 per cent of the expenses were funded from outside sources. Now funding of expenditures from own resources is the predominant source. Tuition fees alone cover between 60 to 70 per cent of the costs. This is a relatively high ratio in comparison to some international universities (see Box 3.1). Current tuition fees are high by Pakistani standards: USD7,500 a year. Therefore, LUMS cannot afford to transfer a larger burden on to the students, hence the importance of the endowment fund.

Another factor of success is the arm's length arrangement that has been maintained between the management committee and the university administration (although there are issues, as discussed later). Unlike some other academic institutions in Pakistan and elsewhere, it is not a family-run institution. This has largely allowed management to take day-to-day decisions.

The growing importance of research is also a burgeoning strength of LUMS. In the earlier years, LUMS was almost exclusively a teaching university, with little emphasis placed on research. Over time, more priority was given to research, starting with the tenure of Dr Ahmad Jan Durrani (2008–2011). The university currently encourages research achievements and provides advice on government

Box 3.1: International Experience with Tuition Fees

In a typical year for Shanghai Jiao Tong University (SJTU), tuition fees account for about 20 per cent of total revenues, with the rest coming from government transfers (40 per cent); research income (30 per cent); and other resources (10 per cent).

In the case of Korea's Pohang University of Science and Technology (POSTECH), despite changes in the revenue composition, the university has kept the proportion of tuition fees in total revenue below 10 per cent.

University of Malaya student fees are highly subsidized: only 3 per cent of the 2008 operating budget came from tuition fees. For the National University of Singapore (NUS) tuition income in the same year was about 17 per cent of the operating budget. A comparison of average annual fees for local and international undergraduates and graduate programmes in both universities showed high subsidy levels for local students in University of Malaya, whereas NUS appeared to base its fees for local students more on the principle of cost recovery.

Mexico's Monterray Institute of Technology is a private institution which receives no direct funding from the government. Its funding base comes mostly from tuition fees, revenues generated by a massive lottery, and donations from private individuals and companies.

Source: Altbach, P. and J. Salmi (2011).

policymaking and local economic development. The institution consults with the government and local organizations regarding socio-economic development. To provide a greater incentive to research, there is a relatively low teaching load compared to other local institutions, and sabbatical leave is provided after six years of service. LUMS is now dedicated to producing and disseminating knowledge through research.

In 2010, the university established a new office, the Office of Graduate Studies and Sponsored Research (GSSR), for providing effective assistance to faculty and staff in administering external and internal sponsored research.[2]

The name of the department has since been changed to the Office of Sponsored Programmes (OSP). The main responsibilities of OSP include providing support to research proposals, consulting arrangements, sponsored conferences, workshops, seminars, and other activities linked to sponsored and externally-funded activities. The office ensures that submitted proposals conform to sponsor guidelines and with relevant university policies and procedures.

LUMS offers different types of internal funding opportunities to the faculty, such as the Faculty Initiative Fund (FIF), the Faculty Travel Grant (FTG), and other grants which are awarded to various faculty members in all schools.

In addition to these grants, several kinds of funding—from domestic and international donors—are available to researchers. At the national level, major sponsors include the Higher Education Commission (HEC)[3], the National ICT R&D Fund, Pakistan Science Foundation, Pakistan Strategy Support Programme, etc. Major international donors include the Centre for Earthquake Studies (CES), Cleaner Production Institute (CPI), World Wildlife Fund (WWF), the Asia Foundation, International Water Management Institute (IWMI), UNICEF, International

Growth Centre (IGC), DFID, USAID, Citi Foundation, and DAAD Germany.

This shift in focus toward research will be a factor in the rating of the university internationally. Another factor in the rating will be the internationalization of its faculty and staff. The precarious security situation of the country inhibits a flow of foreign faculty and students. In the past, there have been foreign students from Central Asian countries, Nepal, Bangladesh, and China, and a few foreign faculty members. However, the deteriorating security situation, especially since 2007, has virtually brought an end to this flow. To compensate for this low foreign intake, student exchange programmes have been the focus of several collaborative agreements that LUMS has established with educational institutions all over the world; however, substantial internationalization will have to await an improvement of the country's security situation.

A factor of importance is that outputs and outcomes are routinely measured and assessed. This is a hallmark of successful universities (see Box 3.2). In addition to teaching evaluations, some of the indicators measured are research produced and published in reputable journals, teaching material developed, case studies developed, research funding generated, consultancy work undertaken, conferences attended, training undertaken, etc. All this is documented and appraised annually and periodically by the Faculty Appointment and Promotion Committee (FAPC)/school tenure committees, based on which decisions on the hiring and promotion/tenure of the faculty are taken.

Box 3.2: Performance Measures and Indicators Used at Two Universities

A clear vision of the institution's mission and goals, and a clearly articulated translation of the vision into concrete programmes and targets have played a critical role in guiding Shanghai Jiao Tong University's development. The university first proposed its mission and goals in 1996 and has designed and undertaken strategic planning accordingly. The Office of Strategic Planning, established in 1999 is responsible for directing the institution's development and for accountability and evaluation. The efforts have been implemented at two levels in SJTU. At the university level, the office benchmarked SJTU with its domestic peers. A range of performance indicators was identified at the university level, including subject areas, faculty structure, student capacity, quality and quantity of publications, citation index, and other factors. At the second level, all schools and departments are required to analyse their own status quo and set up their own policies and performance indicators based on the university's mission and goals.

In the case of the National University of Singapore, the measures for excellence in teaching and research include external university rankings; productivity (research output, international peer-reviewed publications, citations received and average citations per publication); and international recognition of faculty as seen in invitational leadership positions and membership in professional organizations, invitational participation in select conferences and associations, and receipt of achievement awards.

Source: Altback, P. and J. Salmi (2011).

At the same time, the introduction or change in academic policies and procedures follows a rigorous three-tiered process of review, recommendation, and implementation. Policies and procedures are reviewed by relevant faculty standing committees which forward their recommendations to the Faculty Council—the final recommending body. After presentation of any policy change to the Faculty Plenary, its adoption and implementation is approved by the Vice Chancellor, or, in some instances by the Management Committee. In the past year or so, LUMS has made a concerted effort to strengthen its internal processes, and review and document various academic policies and procedures in light of international best practice.

Finally, another strength of LUMS has been the ability to adapt to prevailing circumstances. For example, the adoption of the case study method early on had a very positive effect on the curriculum. Similarly, there was a shift from the three-year undergraduate programme to the four-year programme after they realized that foreign universities did not recognize the three-year programme.

REMAINING ISSUES

By all accounts and under most criteria, LUMS is an outstanding Pakistani university which has established a credible reputation for quality education. As indicated earlier, it is one of only two Pakistani institutions of higher learning that has received the prestigious accreditation of the South Asia Quality Assurance System (SAQS).

Nevertheless there are some issues that LUMS will need to address if it is to maintain its solid reputation.

An issue that raises concern is related to the governance of the institution, more specifically, the role of the five or six-member management committee. The best modern universities exhibit shared governance, with the academic community in control of essential academic decisions and the managers and administrators responsible for resources, facilities, and other administrative matters. This has not always been the case with LUMS. There is a need for the management committee to focus on strategic issues and on ensuring that the university has enough resources to maintain standards and meet its vision. Too often, when tensions on tenure and resources have arisen, the committee has reacted by centralizing decision-making, which has made the situation worse. Also, this committee has no academics on it, depriving it of adequate representation of the views of the faculty. Tensions have developed between the committee and the vice chancellors, which has also seeped to the schools.

Since the management committee did not have the ability to solve emerging problems, there was a high turnover of vice chancellors; between 2001 and 2013, there were four changes of vice chancellors. This is very high turnover compared to some reputable international universities. For example, during the fifty-year period from 1962 to 2012, the National University of Singapore (NUS) had only five vice chancellors. In the case of Mexico's Monterrey Institute of Technology, since it was founded more than sixty years ago, it has had only three rectors and three board presidents. Some tough decisions need to be taken by LUMS' leadership on the role and responsibilities of the management committee, the vice chancellors and the deans.

Another challenge for LUMS as a successful institution is to maintain its standards during times of expansion. During its formative years, LUMS' leadership was nimble and successful in addressing issues and raising funds. Faculty was given the space and initiative to perform its role, but there was no compromise on quality. There was openness among faculty, but this was not institutionalized, and as LUMS started to expand, 'zero-sum tensions' started to develop among schools for resources and priorities. Leadership encountered problems in solving these emerging problems.

Expansionary policies have also led to some growing pains. While the addition of new schools and the availability of sufficient financial aid have made the university accessible to many, the adjustment process has not been without hiccups. In terms of undergraduate academic curriculum, LUMS has followed a liberal arts model where students take a range of courses across disciplines and then subsequently major in a particular subject or discipline. In fact LUMS has been a pioneer in Pakistan in high quality undergraduate education which is broad-based. With the emergence of four new schools and various disciplines with varied pedagogical imperatives, the challenge has been to maintain a sufficiently broad-based education while not compromising on the level of rigour and depth in a particular field.

The rapid expansion has also put constraints on the available physical infrastructure, For example, while there has been an increase in the number of classrooms and faculty, there has been a less than proportional increase in the number of common resources, such as dining centres, computer labs, dormitories, libraries, etc.

Finally, the External Advisory Board generally assesses each school and provides a report to the management committee. However, the university as a whole is not subjected to this assessment. There is, therefore, a silo approach which lacks an integrated assessment. There is need for a holistic internal and external evaluation, which is not done currently. Also, data is scattered, and history is not well chronicled, which prevents learning from lessons of experience. This calls for an annual performance report, which needs to be shared with the public.

Notwithstanding these surmountable problems, LUMS continues to have an excellent reputation in the country and the region. It also retains most of the values that its early leadership instilled in the institution.

4

Institute of Business Administration

Introduction

Located in Karachi, Pakistan's largest city, the Institute of Business Administration (IBA) is a good example of a successful Pakistani higher learning institution in the field of management and business administration. Despite being publicly-owned, and notwithstanding its ups and downs, IBA remains a success story.

This chapter focuses on IBA's historical evolution, its relative decline in the late 1990s, its stabilization during the early 2000s, and its resurgence since 2008. This chapter also summarizes the key determinants of the performance of IBA and concludes with some of the challenges that the institution faces in its evolution toward a world-class seat of learning.

Background

Established in 1955, during the formative years of Pakistan, it was the first business school established on the US-MBA model. It also has the distinction of being the first business school established outside of North America. It was set up with collaboration and assistance from Pennsylvania

University's Wharton School of Business. Support also came from the University of Southern California to help set up several facilities at the institute and assist in the assignment of several prominent American professors to IBA. Course content, curriculum, pedagogical tools, and assessment and testing methods were developed under the guidance of reputed scholars from the two universities. Expenditures for this support were covered largely by the United States Agency for International Development (USAID). IBA did not have a charter until 1994, so it was a department of Karachi University until then. In that year, IBA became an independent degree-awarding institution.

In its earlier years, IBA offered graduate programmes only for day scholars. In 1957, an evening programme in graduate studies was launched to serve the needs of a growing number of working executives and managers who were interested in furthering their careers through part-time business studies. In 1982, a three-year BBA (Honours) programme was introduced, which has since been upgraded to a four-year BBA programme. The institute's graduate programme includes executive MBAs for banking and financial services professionals, corporate managers, and public sector executives. These programmes require significant and relevant work experience in the industry, resulting in a high average age of the class—upwards of thirty years. The success of the institute is manifested by some of its 9,500 alumni who have gone on to become leaders in industry, government, and academia in Pakistan, as well as abroad. In turn, the alumni play the role of development coaches under the Student Development Programme, which helps more than seven hundred newcomers to identify and address their weaknesses.

In 1983, IBM's office in Pakistan collaborated with IBA to develop and establish the Centre for Computer Studies (now referred to as the Faculty of Computer Science). It offers BBA (MIS), BS (Economics and Mathematics), MBA (MIS), BS and MS (Computer Science, Software Engineering and Information Technology), and PhD programmes.

When IBA was established, it had its only campus, called the University Campus, at Karachi University. Later, another campus—the City Campus—was established for evening studies. The City Campus now holds both morning and evening classes.

Since 2009, private foundations, philanthropists, and corporate sectors have helped IBA in upgrading, modernizing, and expanding its existing facilities and constructing thirteen new buildings, a sports complex, a student centre, residential facilities, etc.

Student enrolment has gradually increased, with the number of students growing from about 1,810 in 2008–09 to about 2,900 in 2013–14 (Table 4.1). A decline in the enrolment occurred starting 2011–12 due to the requirement of two year's work experience as the eligibility criterion for admission to the MBA programme.

Table 4.1: Anatomy of the Student Body, 2013–14

	Number	% Male	% Female
Total Students	2,919	60	40
Undergraduate	2,181	53	47
Graduate	463	75	25
Executive Programme	275	90	10

Note: The ratio of female students in total declines significantly after undergraduate degree.

Source: IBA Annual Reports.

Commensurate with the growing student body, the size of the full-time faculty has grown from 23 in 2000 to 90 in 2013, as indicated in Table 4.2.

Table 4.2: Full-Time Faculty Strength, 2000–2013

Year	PhD		Masters		Total	Male	Female
	Foreign	Local	Foreign	Local			
2000	4	4	3	12	23	17	6
2008	18	5	17	22	62	39	23
2012	24	8	27	18	77	48	29
2013	31	9	29	21	90	59	31

Source: IBA Annual Reports.

In terms of sources of funding for the operating costs, the share of tuition fees has gradually increased over time, from about 40 per cent in FY 2007–08 to 51 per cent in FY 2011–12. The interest on IBA reserves and endowments declined from 25 per cent to 18 per cent over the same period, as did government grants (See Table 4.3).

Table 4.3: Sources of Gross Operating Receipts, FY 2007-FY 2013

Source	FY 2007/08	FY 2008/09	FY 2009/10	FY 2010/11	FY 2011/12	FY 2012/13	Budget FY 2013/14
Tuition fees	40	42	49	53	51	54	54
Interest on reserves & endowments	25	38	25	20	18	11	8
Government grants	21	15	16	17	19	13	12
Scholarship grants	5	4	4	3	5	4	4
Other income	9	1	6	7	7	18	22
Gross operating receipts	100	100	100	100	100	100	100

Source: IBA Annual Reports and interviews.

Finally, IBA's admission policy is need-blind. The outreach effort for reaching promising but financially-handicapped students is administered through two programmes: The National Talent Hunt Programme (NTHP) and the Sindh Talent Hunt Programme (STHP). Launched in 2004, NTHP primarily targets financially-constrained students from backward areas of Balochistan, Punjab, Sindh, Federally Administered Tribal Areas (FATA), Khyber Pakhtunkhwa, and the Northern Areas. Almost one-fourth of the student body receives full or partial funding. Promising students from poor backgrounds are encouraged to apply. They are prepared in English, mathematics, and communications skills for the entry examination through a six-month programme, after which the candidates take the IBA examination. Out of roughly 30–40 applicants under this programme in 2012–13, roughly seven or eight were accepted, while the remainder—given their acquired preparation—found acceptance at other good Pakistani universities. Over the past ten years (2004–13), seventy students have been admitted from the two hundred and twenty students trained. The STHP was launched in 2009 with the objective of preparing talented students from the rural areas of Sindh for the aptitude test for BBA/BS degree courses. STHP is a fully funded programme jointly financed by IBA and the Sindh Government.

TURBULENT YEARS

IBA started operating successfully since its birth in 1955, with solid backing from US institutions—Wharton School and University of Southern California—and also with strong support from the local business community. It was able to attract foreign faculty and students. Its discipline and rigour were outstanding, with merit-based selection of faculty and staff.

However, from the mid-1990s through the early 2000s, the institute underwent a relative decline in its standing, as happens from time to time with many universities (see Box 1 for the example of Nigeria's University of Ibadan). Several factors accounted for IBA's decline.

First, the deteriorating security situation in Karachi inhibited the internationalization of IBA, with foreign faculty and students staying away. Prior to the 1980s, it was typical for foreign students, especially from South and East Asia and the Middle East, to come to IBA. This changed as crime and violence engulfed Karachi. International conferences at IBA attracted very few foreign participants. Even domestically, some students and faculty moved to Lahore and Islamabad where the security situation was not as turbulent.

A second factor was the springing up of universities in the gulf countries that offered much better salaries to their faculty and other staff. Today, Dubai hosts almost fifty universities, while Qatar has established the Education City, a location that houses several US colleges, including Carnegie Mellon, Cornell, Georgetown, and Northwestern. There is also the New York University of Abu Dhabi (NYU Abu Dhabi), including the university's new Saadiyat Island campus. Saudi Arabia has also decided to emphasize higher education, with the completion of Princess Nourah bint Abdulrahman University (PNU) in Riyadh—a 2,000 acre site and the largest all-female university in the world.

Most of these Gulf institutions have built state-of-the-art research facilities to attract faculty and students from abroad.

A third factor was the rapid turnover of the leadership of IBA during the period from 1995 to 2002. During this seven-year period, five deans/directors served the institute, with an average tenure of only one and a half years. By comparison, the first dean/director of IBA served for

Box 4.1: The Rise, Decline, and Resurgence of Nigeria's University of Ibadan

The University of Ibadan is frequently referred to as Nigeria's 'premier university' and the 'first and the best'. It is an excellent example of a university that started with a great deal of promise, fell on bad times, but re-emerged as a successful institution.

Its rise

- It was helped considerably by its early affiliation with the University of London, it was almost an external campus and a replica of the latter.
- The management consciously aimed at attracting high-calibre staff. Recruitment and advancement of staff (academic, technical, and administrative) followed strictly British standards. Student recruitment was fiercely competitive.
- The University of London label, the preponderance of British lecturers and professors, the London-determined and London-controlled curricula, and the highly competitive and elitist student admissions procedures resulted in enhanced stature of the university all over the Commonwealth countries.
- Staff composition was truly international, encouraging a rich academic and social culture of the university. In the early years of the university, the staff had only a handful of Nigerian academics.
- Physical and pedagogical facilities were of a high standard.
- Student members were relatively small, which meant manageable teacher-student ratios.
- Establishment and broadening of academic links with foreign institutions and foundations (mainly the Ford, Rockefeller, and Nuffield Foundations) resulted in funding of programmes and facilities and the promotion of staff development initiatives.
- Staff development was given priority to ensure that academic staff remained up-to-date in their disciplines through attendance at conferences, research and travel grants, and

sabbatical leave arrangements with internationally reputed centres of excellence.

Factors behind the fall—1967 to 1999

- The university's disturbed years coincided with a period of grave challenges to the building of the Nigerian nation. The period was marked by the civil war of 1967–70, and its aftermath of prolonged military rule with a civilian interlude (1979–83). The political turmoil in the country profoundly affected the university.
- The university underwent a heavy exodus of academic and other staff members of Igbo origin. This impact was further aggravated by the departure of a sizeable number of non-Nigerian staff members because of security threats.
- The military dictatorship also led to disputes over university autonomy and academic freedom during the 1970s when the military increased its control of the university.

Efforts to revitalize the university

- Nigeria's 15 years of uninterrupted civilian rule since 2000 has given the University of Ibadan a renewed lease on academic life. Autonomy and accountability increased, although financial autonomy still remains elusive with the federal government's decisions to forbid charging of tuition fees.
- More stress was placed on strategic planning. A strategic plan to internationalize the university was produced in 2008 for the period 2009–14, which serves as a roadmap for achieving the vision of a world-class institution with academic excellence geared towards meeting societal needs.
- Based on the latest financial statistics for the university, the average funding by government is 85 per cent, average funding from student charges 1 per cent, donations 1 per cent, and internally generated revenues 12 per cent. The university's expenditures always exceeded available resources until 2005/06 when, for the first time in recent years, expenditures were

less than revenues. This reflects the efforts being made to implement the strategic objective of an efficient, accountable, and sustainable financial management system.

Remaining challenges

- An issue of prime concern is the financial dependence of the university on government donations, which hampers the overall autonomy of the university.

- A pressing issue is the size of its non-academic staff. The university has rebalanced this over the years, but there are still three non-academic staff members for every academic staff member.

- Another challenge is the international composition of academic staff. For example, out of 1,197 academic staff, only 4 are non-Nigerians.

Source: Adapted from Materu, P. et al. (2011).

eighteen and a half years, from 1954 to 1972. This rapid turnover of top leadership resulted in an absence of a long-term vision for the institute, and a disconnect between senior management and the staff.

Another factor was that during this period, serious reputational damages occurred. Corruption crept in. The 2001 leak of examination papers was a major blow to the institute's reputation. Suddenly, an institute known for its discipline and integrity was exposed as any other entity within a corruption-ridden society.

A fifth factor was the absence of domestic competition prior to the establishment, in Pakistan, of the Lahore

University of Management Sciences (LUMS) and other prestigious and competitive educational institutions. A sense of complacency had spread through IBA's system. Desperately needed infrastructure was not provided. Even the limited funds available were not utilized for upgrading building and information technology facilities.

Yet another reason for the downturn was the weakening link with local industry. The technological and entrepreneurial demands of the industry were not fulfilled, and in parallel, donations from the industry to IBA dried up.

Finally, research at the institute was not as interdepartmental as it should have been. For example, the faculty of computer sciences did not have enough joint projects with other disciplines, such as marketing, finance, management, and economics, for operational benefits of research to aid the country.

All the above factors led to excessive focus on day-to-day firefighting, absence of a viable strategic plan, mistrust between the board and management, and a despondency among the faculty and other staff. This situation was further aggravated by the severe security problems endemic to Karachi.

Recent Resurgence of IBA

By late 1990s and early 2000s, IBA was in a major decline. Discipline was floundering. Faculty was migrating out of the institution. Research was weak. Board meetings were rare, and the executive committee took decisions in a non-transparent and top-down manner. Adding to these difficulties was the deteriorating security situation in Karachi. IBA stopped attracting foreign faculty, and international conferences at IBA attracted few foreign participants.

The board finally realized the magnitude of the problem and changed the management of the institute. The new dean/director, Mr Danishmand, steadied the decline during his six-year tenure and helped rebuild the reputation of IBA. But the real turnaround took place after Dr Ishrat Husain was appointed the dean/director in 2008. Highly respected in the country for his successful stint as the governor of the State Bank of Pakistan, and internationally recognized as a scholar and strong manager, he set about addressing the key issues confronting IBA.

Dr Husain provided the leadership that IBA desperately needed at a critical time for the institution. He developed, in a participative manner, a longer-term vision for IBA. He instituted regular weekly meetings in a collegial atmosphere of the executive committee, where decisions were made as a unified team. He developed the IBA Code Book, which incorporates in a single document all the relevant rules and regulations at IBA and which is updated regularly. He improved the working conditions and salaries of the staff. Also, given his reputation with the private sector in Karachi, he was able to raise large donations for upgrading the badly depreciated building and information technology infrastructure. In short, he brought a change of culture and excitement in the institution.

The leadership provided at a critical time had a significant positive impact on IBA. The institute's vision of becoming one of the top ten business schools in South Asia was fulfilled when, in 2011, it received the accreditation of the South Asia Quality Assurance System (SAQS). IBA is now one of only two business schools in Pakistan (the other is LUMS) to have achieved this distinction. The new vision is to be one of the top hundred universities in the world, which would be helped by accreditation of the Association to Advance Collegiate Schools of Business (AACSB). This ranking has several criteria: excellent faculty, outstanding students, state-of-the-art infrastructure, high employability of its students, and high quality of its executive development education.

The above vision led to a three-pronged strategy. First, an audit of all academic programmes was undertaken and some of the programmes were revamped. Secondly, there was increased focus on faculty development. In 2007, there were nineteen PhDs in the faculty. By 2013, this had risen to 40, roughly 45 per cent of the full-time faculty. Most of these (31 out of 40) had PhDs from foreign universities. In some cases, faculty was laid off and new faculty was brought in who were offered good financial packages. The average monthly salary and benefits of an IBA employee multiplied 2.6 times between July 2008 and June 2013, from PKR43,000 to PKR110,000 per month, far higher than the cost of living increase during this period. Student evaluation of faculty was instituted. The faculty was encouraged to do more research and publish papers in recognized journals. This is a change from IBA's status as essentially a teaching institution. As an incentive, the teaching course load is being reduced to enable research.

Thirdly, a large-scale effort was initiated to improve infrastructure. Apart from upgrading the existing infrastructure, new buildings had to be built. USAID had promised to finance some of the expenditures, but when it backed off because of changing country priorities, the leadership went to Aman Foundation, Mahvash and Jehangir Siddiqui Foundation, and Abdul Razzak Tabba Group. Capital expenditures increased from PKR171 million in FY 2008–09 to PKR1,251 million in FY 2013–14 (see Table 4.4). During the five-year period from 2008 to 2012, IBA completed nineteen projects, including renovations of nine existing buildings and an additional ten new facilities. The infrastructure work had largely been completed by early 2015 at a total cost of over USD25 million. This expansion of the physical and information communication and technology of IBA during the past five years has established the base for the diversification of its programmes in new areas besides consolidating the existing programmes. It has also laid a solid infrastructure base for adapting the institution's strategic development goals, improving teaching and research quality, and meeting the expanded enrolment.

Table 4.4: Trends in Capital Expenditures, 2008–2014 (PKRMillions)

Year	Amount
FY 2008–09	171
FY 2009–10	651
FY 2010–11	408
FY 2011–12	780
FY 2012–13	953
FY 2013–14 (budgeted)	1,251

Source: IBA Annual Reports.

REASONS BEHIND THE SUCCESS OF IBA

A critically important factor for the success of IBA as an institution has been the sustained leadership during its formative 'golden years' during the 1950s and early 1960s as well as its more recent visionary and proactive leadership. As the first business school in Pakistan—and indeed the first outside of North America—it was blessed with competent management that stayed for sufficient time in office to provide the continuity needed in the early years. For example, during the almost thirty-year period, 1954–1984, only three deans/directors held office. As indicated earlier, IBA fell on difficult times in the late 1990s and early 2000s, but since 2002—and more specifically since 2008—the institution has had a remarkably successful leadership.

Apart from its leadership, an important success factor for IBA has been its rigorous selection procedures, both for students and its faculty; the institute has always maintained a merit-based system, being selective in enrolment. For example, in 2011–12, some 2,250 students applied for BBA, and only 469 (roughly 20 per cent) were selected. It has a strong disciplinary system, and examinations are always held on time, a remarkable achievement for an institution in strife-ridden Karachi. Students are regularly mentored, and are paired with faculty members for continued guidance. To expand their horizons, students are offered exchange programmes with countries such as Malaysia, China, Singapore, and the USA. Symptomatic of its concern for receiving good entering students, when the institution decided to require a mandatory two-year work experience for its MBA applicants, and there was a significant impact on the intake as well as on revenues, IBA management decided to persist with this work requirement.[1] The good quality of IBA graduates and its strong alumni network ensures relatively easy employability for IBA graduates. Some 83 per cent of BBA holders and 91 per cent of MBA holders in 2012 were employed or pursued higher education (see Table 4.5).

Table 4.5: Employment Status of BBA and MBA Graduates, 2012

	BBA		MBA	
	Number	% of batch	Number	% of batch
Employed	170	74%	42	87%
Higher education	21	9%	2	4%
Unemployed	26	11%	2	4%
Not seeking employment	14	6%	2	5%
Total	231	100%	48	100%

Source: IBA Annual Report, 2012.

A great deal of stress is placed on the quality of faculty. Clear guidelines and benchmarks are established for faculty selection. Qualifications are reviewed, presentation to the faculty is required, and an interview with the dean is arranged. Student evaluation of teachers is considered important, and consistently poor evaluations can be problematic for the faculty member. Faculty development is supported, including through participation in domestic and foreign conferences, forums, and symposiums. Staff members are required to go abroad for exposure to international experience. IBA also ensures that faculty who return from training, workshops, or conferences abroad share and disseminate the knowledge they gained with the rest of the faculty. These sessions are arranged by the institute's Quality Enhancement Cell. All this is in addition to relatively good remuneration for the staff.

There is continued focus on improving the case study method through a mixed strategy: combining class teaching with case analysis. To improve the environment, experts have been invited from the Global Business Schools Network (GBSN), LUMS, and Haas Business School, who interacted with IBA faculty and trained them in teaching case studies.

There is also a continued pressure on IBA to perform well from other competitive educational institutions in the country. Rankings of the Higher Education Commission (HEC), under which IBA is second only to LUMS, are taken seriously, with a push toward greater focus on research.[2]

This old, well-established institution, which has been in business for sixty years, appeals to middle-class families who cannot afford to send their children abroad for higher education. Tuition fees at the end of 2013 were around USD2,000 a year. This compares to tuition fees of USD7,500 at LUMS and USD10,000 at Habib University in Karachi.

Financial sustainability seems well assured with the share of tuition fees in total receipts increasing from around 40 per cent in 2007–08 to 51 per cent in 2011–12. Reliance on government grants, while important (about 16 per cent of total), is not the main source of income. Also, increased enrolment will help improve the financial sustainability of IBA. The upgraded infrastructure will allow for expansion of enrolment. As new undergraduate programmes such as BSc in accounting, finance, and social sciences have been added to the curriculum, the projected number of students by end 2015 is likely to rise to 3,000, almost 50 per cent higher than the 2010 level. This additional enrolment should yield revenues that will keep up with the pace of operational expenditures.

Finally, on operational autonomy, despite being a public institution, it has remained immune to government interventions. It has an independent board of directors with members from both the public and private sectors.

REMAINING ISSUES

Despite its period of turmoil, IBA remains one of the top educational institutions in Pakistan. However, it does have to address some issues to meet its next objective of being placed among the top hundred universities in the world. The following are some of the remaining concerns. This list is by no means exhaustive.

1. **Balance between teaching and research**: Historically, IBA has been a teaching institution. To be considered a successful research institution, it will need to place a greater emphasis on research, which carries an important weight in HEC's ranking criteria. However, this balancing of teaching and research will need to be managed well, so that the traditionally strong teaching aspect is not degraded. IBA's adjustment of teaching course load to allow more research is commendable. To get a high rating on annual assessments, faculty members need to do research. Being a good teacher alone is no longer enough. If there is no research undertaken in one or two years, it can become problematic for the faculty member. A monitoring system is being developed to track the research record of the faculty. IBA can be involved more actively in giving policy advice to the federal and provincial governments, as well as the private sector, in areas of its comparative advantage. In particular, the computer science faculty needs to cater more to the technology needs of the local industry. Now that the infrastructure and information technology base has been completed, IBA should encourage and reward faculty members

and students for quality papers published in top international journals in relevant fields.

2. **Increasing internationalization**: Internationalization has a positive impact on the learning environment at a university. The degree of internationalization is also a benchmark for university rankings. For a number of reasons, most prominently the security situation in Karachi, the number of foreign faculty and students at IBA is negligible. This was not always the case. Prior to the 1980s, the institute attracted students and faculty from the US, Malaysia, Australia, China, and the Middle East. For IBA to get an international ranking, it must have a reasonable number of international students. An opening has been made by IBA in sending students to China, India, Bangladesh, Malaysia, Turkey, and France, but more effort and financial support to outstanding students will be needed. There has also been a gradual shift from domestic to foreign events (conferences, seminars, forums, and symposiums). The share of foreign events in total events increased from 17 per cent in 2009–10 to 30 per cent in 2010–2011 and 41 per cent in 2011–12.

3. **Improving faculty quality**: Once again, the unsettled political and security situation in Karachi renders it difficult to hire and retain quality staff. Competition from other Pakistani higher education institutions, and also Middle East universities, is strong. Matching faculty remuneration will be a costly proposition.

Attracting expatriate Pakistani academics from abroad would be one possibility, but there are not enough willing Pakistani scholars who wish to return, and there are not enough in the fields of finance, marketing, and accounting. One approach would be to send IBA's faculty abroad on a more systematic basis for greater exposure.

To summarize, IBA has had its ups and downs, but it continues to remain one of the most outstanding academic institutions in Pakistan, and a good example of an entity that manages to perform well as a public entity in a hostile security environment.

5

Motorway Police

INTRODUCTION

It is universally accepted that corruption has a debilitating impact on the economic development and social fabric of a society. Citizens around the world face administrative corruption in their daily contact with public services. In many developing countries, administrative corruption places a heavy burden on the time and resources of individuals and companies. It also leads to dissatisfaction with public services and undermines trust in public institutions. Often it is the poor and the vulnerable who suffer the most.

Corruption is generally seen as a product of traditional local culture and, as such, inevitable. Political leaders with vested interests exploit this perception of the citizens as an excuse for inaction and for indulging in corruption. Globally there is an overwhelming evidence of reform failures and unmet expectations in this area. And yet, there is also ample evidence that no amount of resistance to anti-corruption measures is sufficient to preclude success if there are the right incentives, sustained discipline, honest and dedicated leadership, and, more generally, a change of culture.

In this chapter, we examine how success was achieved in the operations of the Motorway Police of Pakistan, even though generally the police force has been one of the most corrupt institutions in the country, especially at the lower levels. According to the 2013 Transparency International Report, the police sector was observed as the most corrupt in Pakistan.[1]

BACKGROUND

Less than two decades ago, the traffic culture on Pakistan's highways was marked by a total disregard for traffic rules, an extremely feeble enforcement apparatus, and a very high incidence of accidents. Every year, some 7,000 people lost their lives and another 75,000 were injured in road accidents.[2] When there were traffic infringements, the rich and influential got away, while the poorer citizens were asked to pay, even in cases when they had not broken the law.

In response to this chaotic and corrupt situation, the Pakistan Motorway Police was established by the government in 1997 to police the country's newly constructed motorway network, starting with the Islamabad-Lahore Motorway (M2). Later, in mid-2001, it was also assigned the additional responsibility of patrolling Pakistan's national highways, starting with Pakistan's longest (Karachi-Peshawar) national highway (M5). With the addition of these new responsibilities, the name of the agency was changed to National Highways and Motorway Police (NH&MP), which is now responsible for enforcement of traffic and safety laws and security and recovery on Pakistan's National Highways and Motorway network.

The NH&MP is headquartered in Islamabad and is headed by an inspector general of police (IGP) who is assisted by seven deputy inspectors general (DIGs), each in charge of a separate branch. The total force of about 6,000 consists of about 5,000 uniformed staff and 1,000 non-uniformed staff. A superintendent of police (SP), who reports to a DIG, is responsible for 250 officers, and an assistant/deputy SP manages about 60 officers.

The following are the key objectives of NH&MP:

1. to control traffic violations on motorways and national highways;

2. to educate road users;

3. to launch road safety campaigns to increase awareness among the motorists;

4. to ensure safety and provide assistance to road users and;

5. to treat road users respectfully and fairly but firmly to uphold ethical practices at all times.

NH&MP is adequately equipped with the latest equipment, such as ProVida 2000 (VASCAR), which is a radar fitted with video and not only detects speed but also has a printer which gives a picture of the vehicle along with the prescribed and actual speeds; hand-held radar/laser guns; video/still cameras; first aid boxes; communications systems;

Weber hydraulic cutters as rescue equipment in case of accidents; and night vision speed checking devices. Modern patrol and rescue vehicles are also part of the equipment.

Funding for the organization comes from the federal budget. Revenues from ticket collection go to the federal budget, which then allocates funds to it. Some 50 per cent of the organization's budget is covered by traffic tickets issued.

Prior to the operationalization of NH&MP in 1997, all the officers were selected from within the existing police setups in the country, and an extensive training programme was prepared for them to bring them up to international standards of motorway/expressway policing. Instruction was imparted by foreign and local instructors. Local training was given at a police college in Sihala. To complement this, experts from UK and Nordic countries were invited who, together with local experts, trained NH&MP officers in advanced driving skills and management of different types of incidents. Some trainees were also sent to South Wales Police, UK, and German Police in Kiel. Furthermore, services of armed forces were utilized for advanced driving skills, particularly for motorcycles. To customize the training to the specific needs of the organization, a training college was set up at Sheikhupura to train newly-selected officers in all aspects of motorway operations.

The NH&MP homepage has a travel updates section which provides hourly updates on weather and road conditions on various parts of the highways and motorway network.

WHY IS THE MOTORWAY POLICE CONSIDERED A SUCCESS STORY?

In a short life of about eighteen years, the Motorway Police has established for itself an enviable reputation in the country of being a success story. It has created a 'new culture of policing with a clean image'.[3] It enforces the law equally to all motorists regardless of their position in society, and it does away with the VIP culture so heavily entrenched in Pakistani society. It is highly appreciated and recognized by the public for its efficiency, honesty, and ability to take firm action with a smiling face. Its emergency helpline and regular reports on weather and road conditions on various portions of the highways and motorways are deemed helpful. Motorists on the highways and motorways who need help with their automobiles are served well by NH&MP. It provides 1800–1900 'helps' per day to road users. There has also been a decrease of 70 per cent in fatal and non-fatal accidents over the last decade. Highway crime has also decreased, by one account by 95 per cent.[4] As a result of effective crime control, a large number of stolen vehicles have been recovered. In some instances (for example, in the Nooriabad Industrial Estate on the Super Highway between Karachi and Hyderabad), effective crime control has led to increased industrial activity. Its integrity has been well summarized by the World Bank: 'With regard to petty and middling corruption, the consensus has been that there is hardly any arm of government which does not suffer acutely from corruption, with the exception of the Motorway Police'.[5]

Because of its success, the network has been expanded from Islamabad to Murree, and is also being replicated in selected urban centres in Punjab, such as Lahore, Gujranwala, Faisalabad, Rawalpindi, and Multan.

REASONS FOR SUCCESS

By most accounts, the Motorway Police of Pakistan is a success story and an example of how a culture change can be inculcated to curtail corruption, boost performance, develop a service culture, and establish legitimacy.

Equally important is the fact that the change was effected without any dramatic reduction of the workforce as, for example, was done in the case of Georgia, where all the traffic police were fired with one stroke and a new force was recruited (see Box 5.1). The reform began with officers being handpicked from all provinces, who then underwent intensive training and participated in motivational programmes with a focus on transforming the police force into a 'true public servant'. What followed was the implementation of a multifaceted programme that affected the desired culture change.

The following were some of the factors behind the successful reform of the Motorway Police:

1. **Eliminating Corruption**: Special initiatives were taken to avoid the prevalent corruption in the national police force. A substantial number of ill-reputed officers were suspended and removed from service. Standard operating procedures were put in

Box 5.1: Chronicle of Georgia's Patrol Police Reform

In early 2000s, Georgia's police system was riddled with corruption. To make up for their poor salaries—when they were paid at all—many worked for organized crime or were involved in drug dealing. They also accused citizens of breaking the law—regardless of whether they had or not—and then pocketed the fines. Traffic police were almost always involved in victimizing citizens. On a short drive, one would invariably be hauled up at least twice and asked for a fine. This system of corruption resulted in a vicious cycle in which money never reached state coffers, salaries were not paid on a regular basis, and police turned to crime to make money.

Traffic police in particular were consistently rated among the most corrupt public officials in the country. A survey in 2000 concluded that when stopped by traffic police, motorists were asked for bribes in seven out of ten contacts. In the same survey, public officials, enterprises and households alike ranked the honesty of traffic police among the lowest of any public official.

Reform began by severing the ties between the government and organized criminals. It went on to create a whole new cadre of patrol police. In one of the boldest moves of the reform, all 16,000 traffic police were fired. To make the decision palatable, the government provided two months' pay and amnesty from past crimes. Interestingly enough, chaos did not follow; indeed many observers felt that the roads were actually safer without traffic police waving motorists over all the time. A completely new patrol was created. To ensure success, undercover officers were assigned to make sure the new police followed the rules. This sent a strong message to new recruits that the ministry was serious about its code of conduct. A 24-hour hotline was established to enable citizens to complain about police or report about bribe demands or unfair treatment. Video cameras were installed in major cities and along highways giving police and citizens proof of violations. Fines were no longer collected on the spot but paid at commercial banks, thus eliminating opportunities for police to pocket the money.

The result of the reform was a corruption-free police force imbibed with a service culture. Now the police are considered friendly, courteous, well-uniformed and service-oriented. They have been trained to be helpful, and it shows. Trust in the police has been established. According to one survey, 84 per cent of respondents in 2010 had confidence in the police, compared to only 10 per cent in 2003.

Source: World Bank (2012): Fighting Corruption in Public Services, Washington D.C.

place and used, and there is accountability at all levels. An effective vigilance system is in place, and strict supervision and disciplinary action is taken when needed. There are internal checks, and monitoring is undertaken on a daily basis. The adequate compensation package also helps (see below). The incentive for corruption is further diminished by doing away with cash transactions in case of traffic violations. A ticketing system has been adopted, and no documents are seized during a violation of traffic rules by commuters.

2. **Merit-based recruitment**: Selection and recruitment are purely merit-based. Application requirements are explicit, and tests are held simultaneously at all centres. There is video coverage of physical fitness and written tests. There is also a synchronized opening of sealed examination papers. The interview committee

is headed by the inspector general of police, and assignments to new posts are based on merit.

3. **Good working conditions**: There are numerous incentives to attract and retain quality police officers. Pay scales are about 30–40 per cent higher than in other police forces in the country. There are also welfare benefits including free bachelor accommodation, proper mess arrangements, health allowance and indoor/outdoor sports facilities, scholarships, financial assistance for daughters' marriages, burial assistance, welfare petrol pumps, and special employment quotas for children of officers killed in service. For higher efficiency, the force functions in three eight-hour shifts.

4. **Manageable span of control**: There is a manageable span of control, with a superintendent of police managing 250 officers and an assistant/deputy superintendent of police about 60 officers. There is close supervision and effective command and accountability, with senior officers accountable for infringements by subordinates. Also, standard operating procedures are in place and meticulously observed.

5. **Honest force and smart turnout**: The police is honest, corruption-free, courteous, and helpful. Stress is placed on public friendliness rather than punitive policing. There is an emphasis on smart turnout and professionalism, with a distinct uniform.

6. **Empowered and impressive leadership**: There is little interference from any quarter in the performance of duties by the police force. The force has also been fortunate to have effective top leadership, with inspectors general such as Zia ul Hasan and Wasim Kausar, who played a key role in the development of NH&MP.

7. **Effective training**: A great deal of emphasis is placed on traffic education and road safety measures. The training strategy involves SWOT analysis, qualified instructors, modern techniques of instruction, simulation exercises, case studies, familiarity with modern electronic gadgets, and foreign training. Officers were sent in batches to UK and Germany for specialized training, and skilled staff members from the UK police force were invited to train officers in Pakistan. Officers were also trained in first aid techniques, with refresher courses conducted at the end. Special emphasis is given to ensuring that commuters respect lane discipline, seat belt discipline, obeying speed limits and avoiding underage driving.

8. **Modern equipment**: To improve the effectiveness of the police, the latest patrol vehicles and equipment are utilized: patrol cars, radars, night-vision equipment, etc. Thanks to the camera recording and other equipment, there have hardly ever been cases challenged in the court. There are mobile-repair workshops on the Motorway (M2) for public convenience. There are also axel weight controls and

fencing of the Motorway to avoid stray animals from causing accidents.

9. **Doing away with the VIP culture**: There is courteous but firm enforcement of the law without exception. The force has done away with the unequal application of the law. As an example, the number of tickets issued to VIPs increased from 40 in 2000 to 67 in 2001; 276 in 2002; and 310 in 2003.

10. **Noteworthy gender strategy**: Another commendable initiative of the Motorway Police has been its gender strategy, with its emphasis on increasing the representation of women in the organization. A 10 per cent quota in recruitment has been reserved for women in the organization. Besides, a number of courses have periodically been arranged to enhance the capabilities of women police officers. Gender-sensitivity learning has been assimilated into police training as part of the curriculum, with the aim of making NH&MP an equal-opportunity organization.

11. **Other measures to gain public trust**: A department of NH&MP is devoted to corporate social responsibility. It has provided daily assistance to commuters in distress; reunited lost children with their families; provided assistance to internally displaced persons (IDPs) and flood victims; and increased awareness in various capacities for breast cancer, dengue fever, and polio eradication.

Remaining Issues

To ensure further improvement of NH&MP, the following measures will need to be taken:

1. Foreign Training of NH&MP staff in France, Germany, UK and other developed countries should be continued to improve overall performance and skills acquisition in techniques and management. Foreign training was a regular feature until a few years ago when it was discontinued for budgetary reasons.

2. Since the scope of traffic management by NH&MP has been expanded to other highways (Indus Highway, Islamabad-Murree Highway, and Coastal Highway), adequate budgetary provisioning should be ensured for the purchase of equipment, transport, etc. to maintain and enhance the present standards.

3. Professional and experienced police officers should be selected to head the NH&MP. A professional and efficient commander can have a remarkable effect on overall performance and results.

4. The latest equipment should continue to be inducted including night vision, speed-monitoring cameras, recovery vehicles, ambulances, etc. to enhance the effectiveness of the organization.

5. Traffic engineering plays a very important role in preventing road accidents and improving traffic flow. Several 'black spots' on highways have been identified

where several accidents have taken place. Therefore, change of road design, fencing, etc. is needed to prevent road mishaps at these spots.

6. Fencing of highways, as done in most countries, would avert pedestrians from being hit by motorists, especially in populated areas.

7. Educational programmes for road users, and more generally in educational institutions, should be undertaken on a regular basis to enhance traffic education at all levels.

6

Benazir Income Support Programme

INTRODUCTION

Few public entities in Pakistan have fulfilled their established objectives as effectively as the Benazir Income Support Programme (BISP). This programme was launched in July 2008 with the immediate objective of ameliorating the negative effects of slow economic growth, rising food prices, and inflation on the roughly 25 million (15 per cent of the country's population) living in extreme poverty, particularly women, through cash transfers to eligible families (Government of Pakistan 2013). The longer–term objectives of the programme are to meet two of the Millennium Development Goals (MDGs): (i) to eradicate extreme and chronic poverty; and (ii) to empower women.

The programme's novel features include the substitution of cash transfers for transfers in the form of targeted or generalized food subsidies (through price discounts, price controls, in-kind distribution of food items, etc.). This gives beneficiary families complete freedom in their spending decisions. To ensure that the transfers reach the targeted beneficiaries, strict guidelines are utilized for selecting the beneficiaries. Its scale can be gauged by the fact that the federal government's social safety net spending increased from 0.3 per cent of GDP in 2003/04 to 0.9 per cent of GDP in 2011/12 (World Bank, 2012). It is an inclusive programme that has moved away from patronage-based selection of beneficiaries, using explicit, transparent and objective criteria for beneficiary selection, by targeting on the basis of the Poverty Scorecard.

The purpose of this chapter is to examine the factors that lay behind the success of BISP in meeting its goals and also to highlight areas of unfinished agenda and concerns. The chapter concludes that strong government commitment, sufficient delegated responsibility, dedicated management and staff, explicit and objective criteria for support to beneficiaries, and continued financial and technical support of international development agencies helped ensure a successful social protection programme.

With the electoral victory of the Pakistan Muslim League–N (PML–N) Party in mid–2013, and the loss of Pakistan Peoples Party (PPP), which was responsible for the establishment of BISP, there has been a change in leadership, with the head of BISP being replaced.[1] There have also been allegations that BISP management spent excessive amounts on media campaigns and indulged in financial mismanagement and improper procurement. These allegations were investigated by the National Accountability Bureau (NAB) and the new government affirmed its commitment to BISP, nominated a competent person to head the agency, and increased the allocation to BISP.[2] There were further increases in BISP's budget for 2014–15 and 2015–16.

HISTORICAL CONTEXT

Prior to 2008, federal cash transfer programmes—Zakat and Baitul Maal—accounted for the bulk of cash transfers in Pakistan. Zakat was initiated during General Zia ul–Haq's regime in the 1980s as a safety net for 'deserving needy' Muslims (Khan, S. and Qutb, S. 2010). It consists of cash allowances, grants to small businesses and education, health, and marriage related assistance. Baitul Maal, on the other hand, is a tax-financed programme administered through provincial and district branches (Gazdar, H. 2011).

Zakat and Baitul Maal have a number of shortcomings. They lack a transparent mechanism for targeting, frequently resulting in patronage-based allocations. Their coverage is limited. They often include the non-poor and exclude the poorest. They do not provide regular, dependable support, and therefore do not permit households smooth consumption throughout the course of the year nor protect them from unanticipated external shocks.[3] They also face institutional and administrative challenges (Kabeer, N. et al. 2010).

In 2008, the new coalition government led by PPP made a clear break with the past on the approach to social protection and established BISP. There was a shift in focus towards cash transfers as the main source of social protection. At the same time, the amount allocated to cash transfers was increased three-fold in real terms (Bari, F. and Cheema, A. 2012). While the National Social Protection Strategy (NSPS), which had been prepared in 2007, had not been implemented, it became a readily available instrument for policy action in this area.

Activities under the BISP umbrella were initiated with targeted Unconditional Cash Transfer (UCT) amounting to PKR1,000 (roughly USD10, at exchange rate of early 2015) per month to ever-married women in poor households. This amount was increased to PKR1,200 during FY 2013–14 and to a further PKR1,500 during FY 2014–15. Initially, with certain conditions, parliamentarians were given the task of helping identify the beneficiaries. Each member of the National Assembly and Senate was given 8,000 applications and each member of the Provincial Assembly was given 1,000 applications, followed by the application of categorical selection criteria, managed by the National Database Registration Authority (NADRA). However, for better targeting, the BISP Poverty Scorecard (developed with technical assistance from the World Bank) was developed, which is a Proxy Means Test (PMT) aimed at providing an easily measurable proxy for a household's level of poverty. Households having PMT score of 16.17 or below become eligible for BISP benefits. However, it is pertinent to mention that the cut-off of 16.17 is not indicative of the poverty line. Rather, this cut-off was decided on the basis of fiscal space available with the programme at the time of survey. Crucially, within the household, a 'receiver woman' was identified, defined as an ever-married woman having a valid Computerized National Identity Card (CNIC), who is then eligible to receive the cash benefit. Initially disbursements were made through

Pakistan Post, which has a wide outreach even in remote parts of the country. However, in the face of complaints of delays and misappropriation, disbursements were made electronically through smart cards, mobile phone banking, and ATM debit cards. By the end of 2013, more than 4 million women had received these electronic cash instruments. It is expected that up to 7 million will receive these cards and thus be eligible for cash transfers during the next two to three years.

To facilitate the graduation of poor households out of poverty, BISP has also expanded its menu to include initiatives like: Conditional Cash Transfer (CCT),[4] linked to education; health and life insurance; microfinance; and vocational and technical training (Bari, F. and Cheema A. 2012). Its *Waseela–e–Haq* programme provides a loan of up to PKR300,000 with a maturity of fifteen years to a family receiving cash transfers through BISP via computerized random draw. Once the full amount of microfinance is received, the family graduates out of the BISP UCT programme after expiry of the grace period of one year. A microfinance receiving beneficiary is assisted and trained by BISP to set up a small enterprise. Plans are being formalized to transfer this programme to the provinces under the 18th Constitutional Amendment. BISP has initiated a *Waseela–e–Rozgar* programme that provides free vocational training and support to current beneficiaries through the country's vocational training institutes. Again, plans are being finalized to transfer this facility to the provinces. BISP's health and insurance programme, *Waseela–e–Sehat*, is presently being piloted in one district, but it is being expanded to five more districts. For a premium, households are provided with health cards, which can be used to cover expenses up to PKR25,000 per year for the entire family. There is also a life insurance scheme, launched by BISP with the State Life Insurance Corporation that provides insurance coverage of PKR100,000 upon death of the bread winner of the beneficiary family. Finally, its education CCT, *Waseela–e–Taleem*, provides PKR250 per child, per month for up to three children in a family, conditioned on the children attending primary school. This initiative aims to enroll approximately 2 million children in primary schools by 2015–16. As of July 2013, a total of about 75,000 were enrolled in primary schools in five pilot districts, including Malakand, Karachi South, Mirpur, Noshki, and Skardu. To increase the social mobilization under this programme, beneficiary mothers have been organized into 31,000 village committees, with the objective of better understanding of the programme.

STRENGTHS OF BISP

There are several strengths of BISP that make it an important institutional investment for social protection in Pakistan. It is the first social protection programme that is truly country-wide, covering Punjab, Sindh, Balochistan, Khyber Pakhtunkhwa, AJK, and FATA. As a secular programme, it does not discriminate on the basis of religion, allowing it to serve marginalized segments of the country.

The programme represents the first time that women have been targeted specifically as beneficiaries on such a large scale (see below). BISP also provides incentives to the poor and marginalized to get registered under NADRA, thereby strengthening the state's relationship with its citizens.

A bold step away from patronage-ridden programmes, BISP's proxy means testing has institutionalized a transparent and objective selection methodology for potential beneficiaries. The construction of the Poverty Scorecard (PSC) has institutionalized the information needed, and this database can be used by other institutions, organizations, and individuals working on poverty in the country.

Growth of BISP

Since its inception in July 2008, BISP has grown rapidly, and is now the largest single poverty alleviation programme in the country's history (Government of Pakistan, 2013). The number of beneficiaries has increased from 1.7 million households in FY 2008–09 to nearly 5 million by the end of FY 2014–15, and annual disbursements rose from PKR15.8 billion in FY 2008–09 to almost PKR90 billion over the same period (see graphs 6.1 and 6.2). The budgetary allocation for FY 2013–14 was PKR75 million, which was further increased in FY 2015–16. Since its establishment, BISP has disbursed more than PKR160 billion (almost USD1.6 billion). Some 7.7 million beneficiaries have been identified, of whom 5 million are eligible (i.e., have CNICs), while BISP and NADRA are providing assistance to make the remaining 2.2 million also eligible.

Graph 6.1: Number of BISP Beneficiaries

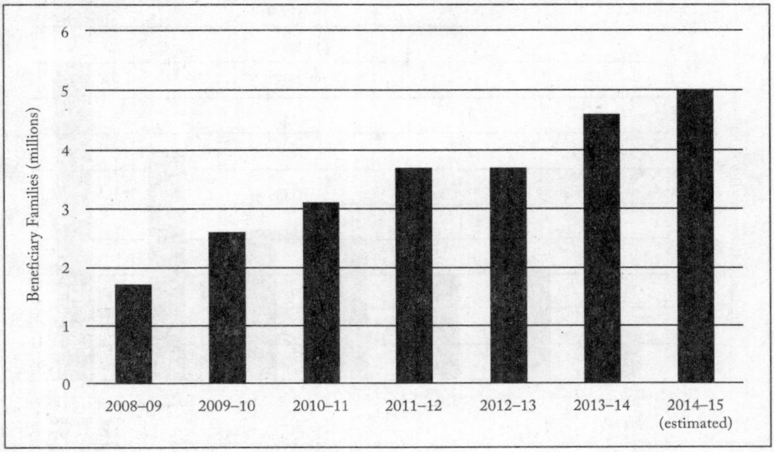

Source: Government of Pakistan, 2014.

IMPACT OF BISP

Cash grants to about 5 million beneficiary families in all provinces and areas of the country have been granted since 2008, directly benefiting at least 20 million people.

This achievement was the result of a shift away from general subsidies towards cash grants. It has thus helped reduce extreme poverty.

Second, the programme is empowering women by disbursing the cash only to female representatives of eligible families. Concurrently, the programme has encouraged women to register with NADRA for the national identity card (CNIC). Since the inception of BISP, a 40-per cent spike has been observed in female registration of CNICs,

Graph 6.2: Annual Cash Grants (in PKR Billions)

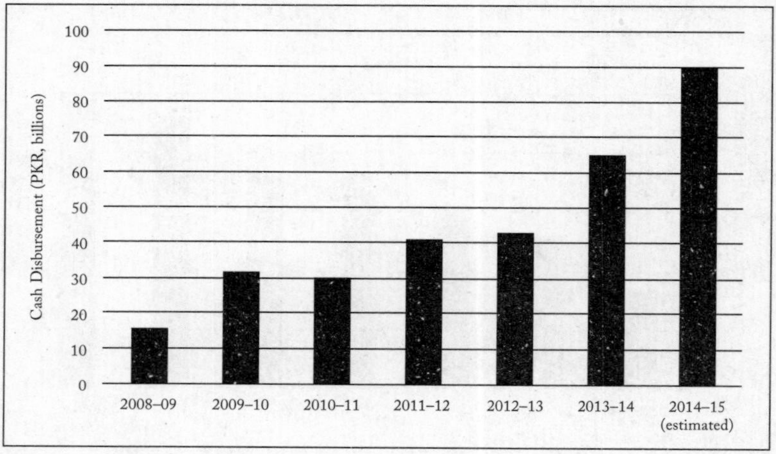

Source: Government of Pakistan, 2014.

which will open avenues for their socio-economic and political empowerment.

Third, BISP has established a credible foundation for a national poverty registry as initial results of spot checks show the accuracy rate of the poverty scorecard survey as 95.4 per cent.

Cash transfers from BISP have also had the following beneficiary effects on various aspects of the poor:

- It has directly raised the household expenditures on a range of items such as food, clothing, healthcare, education, and transport. The regular and predictable cash transfer to the households allows the latter to smooth consumption over time as well as increasing food consumption.

- It has helped improve child nutrition.
- It reduces vulnerability to exogenous shocks. Vulnerable households are prone to adverse exogenous shocks. BISP helps compensate for the lack of formal and informal insurance markets and helps them avoid harmful coping strategies that aggravate the negative effects of the adverse shocks (O'Leary, S. et al. 2011).
- It results in better health and education outcomes. The most commonly cited reason for not accessing health care despite the incidence of illness is that the poor cannot afford consultation. Similarly, despite education being free in Pakistan for children aged five to sixteen years, the most common reason for not enrolling is the expense of education, with the poor households not able to meet the costs of transport, uniforms, books, and stationery. BISP reduces these financial constraints at least to some extent.
- It helps reduce child labour. Child work patterns change in households where there is an increase in income. The CCT mechanism helps reduce child labour, although the cultural practices of children assisting around the house and on fields or with livestock are unlikely to change.

GOVERNANCE AND MANAGEMENT STRUCTURE

The President and the Prime Minister of Pakistan are the chief patron and executive patron of BISP, respectively. They have the authority to appoint the chairperson of BISP, members of the board, and the management of

BISP. The board consists of nine to eleven members, including the chairperson, who are appointed from both governmental and non-governmental organizations. The members of the board meet quarterly to make financial and macro decisions. They also deal with issues of transparency in the organization. The Act establishing BISP also envisages a council comprising of highly distinguished and accomplished national and international figures, that is also appointed by the chief patron and executive patron to mobilize financial resources for the programme and to advise the board on policy matters. However, the BISP council has not been established yet and the programme is run by its board. BISP management handles micro level daily management, including responsibility for the work of BISP's 2,500 employees at headquarters, provincial offices, divisional levels, and tehsil levels.

REASONS FOR SUCCESS

Like most organizations, BISP has its shortcomings (discussed later). However, in the short lifetime of seven years, it has established itself as a successful programme that has helped in targeting financial support to the poorest in Pakistan in an effective and efficient manner. It has achieved international recognition for its rigorous targeting mechanism, innovative design, and transparent systems. Many other countries such as Bangladesh, India, Ghana, Mongolia, Cambodia, and Nepal have indicated their interest in learning from BISP's experience and design for introducing similar social safety net initiatives in their countries.

There are several political, social, economic, and technical factors that account for BISP's success despite the tight budgetary situation and weak institutional framework of Pakistan.

An important success factor has been the strong and widespread political support for BISP in the establishment and continuation of the programme. This support has continued even with changes of government. Even before the establishment of BISP, there was a ground swell of political support for a new social protection system in the country: the document that formed the basis of BISP—the National Social Protection Strategy of 2007—was prepared under the Musharraf regime. During the PPP government, the fact that the programme's name was associated with the assassinated leader of PPP, Benazir Bhutto, ensured strong support from the ruling party, which also made the party determined to 'keep the programme off limits as a source of rent-seeking' even though this led to some delays in the early stages of the programme (Gazdar, H. 2013). The then–president of the country met with the chairperson of BISP twice a month. Also, the fact that PML-N was in coalition at the federal level and was holding the finance portfolio at the time that BISP was being planned allowed a considerable degree of cross-party support for the programme.

The legitimacy of BISP was also enhanced by the fact that it was created through an act of Parliament that was passed unanimously through the National Assembly and the Senate. This strengthened the institutional foundations of social protection in Pakistan (Bari, F. and Cheema, A. 2012). Moreover, parliamentarians were heavily involved in the mechanism of fund transfers to the eligible poor in the early stages of the programme. Subsequently, even though the distribution of funds with the assistance of parliamentarians was curtailed in favor of the NADRA-based and Poverty Scorecard filters, the political support of the legislators continued. Over time, the provincial governments were also brought on board, all of whom signed MOUs with the programme.

Even the change in government from PPP to PML-N in 2013 did not diminish support for the programme. In fact, the new government increased the budgetary support to BISP. Even when an inquiry by the National Accountability Bureau (NAB) was initiated to investigate charges of mismanagement of media related funds, there was no reduction in support from the government.

Apart from strong government and all-parties commitment to the programme, substantial autonomy was delegated to BISP. The programme has its own chairman, and its own board of directors, 50 per cent of whom are from the private sector. The board has played a positive role, especially in areas of finance, audit, and human resource management.

Delegation was also facilitated by the fact that an efficient, youthful, and honest management team was in place that combined good technical and communications skills in the performance of its duties.

An important success factor, with respect to the political economy of the reforms related to BISP, was the setting-up of a transparent, largely apolitical, and effective targeting mechanism. As indicated earlier, the first phase of the targeting exercise involved elected representatives who identified deserving recipients for the cash transfers (Phase 1); this mechanism was replaced by poverty scorecard based targeting (Phase 2). Generally this would be a difficult switch because it is very difficult to remove beneficiaries once they have been selected on political grounds (Gazdar 2013). The relatively smooth transition from Phase 1 to Phase 2 was an important factor in building the legitimacy and therefore the success of the programme.

The programme also has a good grievance mechanism. Offices have been established at the tehsil level, and internet access was assured for grievance reporting. This kept the system responsive to the concerns of the recipients. Spot checks were also carried out, and there was also a process evaluation mechanism.

Rigorous evaluations have been built into BISP's design, including a dedicated unit for monitoring and evaluation. Evaluations are also undertaken by external organizations to enhance credibility. Invaluable insights are provided by these evaluations, which are then built into the design of the programme. To obtain a more balanced assessment of the programme, especially in the case of impact evaluations, both quantitative and qualitative analyses are performed. Three independent firms were hired to conduct spot checks of eligible beneficiaries, evaluate the processes of programme implementation, and carry out a detailed impact evaluation exercise (Government of Pakistan, 2013).

An important strength of BISP was the ability to learn from its mistakes and to strive for better mechanisms. For example, the shift from Phase 1 to Phase 2 in identifying beneficiaries was based on learning the shortcomings of the first phase. Similarly, the disbursement of funds through Pakistan Post was abandoned once its weaknesses were realized, and there was a move to effect disbursements through smart cards, later through mobile phones, and finally through debit cards. Currently around 4.4 million beneficiaries are receiving payments through technology-based payment mechanisms, with the rest receiving payments through the post office. At each stage, lessons were learned and were incorporated into the design of the programme.

A critically important factor in BISP's success was the significant and timely financial and technical support from external donors. There was also an alignment of objectives between the government and the donors. The government was keen to develop a programme that would target the needs of the poor. This was in line with the poverty alleviation objectives of the international development agencies, which were concerned with the incidence of poverty in the country.

The International Development Association (IDA) of the World Bank provided a credit of USD60 million to BISP in 2009. It supported the design of the poverty scorecard, survey of all households in Pakistan, and related activities. The World Bank followed this up with an additional credit of USD150 million for the launch of the co-responsibility cash transfer for the primary school children of BISP's beneficiaries (*Waseela–e–Taleem*). USAID provided a grant of USD85 million as budgetary support for payment of cash benefits to the beneficiaries identified under the poverty-scorecard system. Subsequently, USAID provided additional funding of USD75 million. In 2009, the Asian Development Bank provided a credit of USD150 million for use by BISP to make transfers to beneficiaries identified through the new targeting system. It followed this with a much larger credit of USD430 million in November 2013. Finally, DFID supported BISP's initial activities (test phase targeting survey, process evaluation, spot checks, etc.) and provided a grant of GBP300 million for the CCT programme for primary education of the children of BISP beneficiaries. The reform of social protection has also figured prominently in Pakistan's negotiations with the IMF.

The programme has also been successful in developing and sustaining valuable partnerships with government as well as non-governmental and private organizations, including through sub-contracting arrangements. These organizations include NADRA, Pakistan Post, the Population Census Organization, commercial banks, survey firms, and mobile phone service providers (Gazdar 2013). There are also emerging partnerships being developed with provincial governments. All these partnerships have facilitated the achievement of BISP's programme objectives.

Finally, an important success factor of the programme was its ability to deftly manage the political economy of the changes. This was particularly in evidence in how the leadership of BISP grappled with concerns regarding the duplication of effort with Zakat and Baitul Maal as well as several other provincial cash transfers programmes. The decision by the government to continue Zakat and Baitul Maal programmes rather than to rationalize all cash transfers under one umbrella illustrates the government's and BISP's sensitivity regarding radical organizational reform. There were repeated statements of assurance that these programmes would not be curtailed.

REMAINING ISSUES AND LOOKING AHEAD

An important determinant of BISP's future success will be the extent to which the programme can withstand political considerations especially in the context of changes of government. The 2013 change in government from PPP to PML-N had some impact: the chairperson of BISP was changed and allegations were brought up against the actions of the previous management in terms of excessive expenditures on public relations and mis-procurements. On the other hand, the government appointed a competent and honest replacement for the chairman's post in November 2013 (Enver Baig), who in turn was replaced by Marvi Memon in February 2015. The government also made a further increase in the allocation for 2013–14 to PKR75 billion. The message from the government was that, while it did plan to address any misappropriations that might have occurred in the programme, it accepted ownership of the programme. However, there is no doubt that the frequency of changes of the chairmen is harmful and does not allow them to focus more seriously on the important issues that need to be addressed. BISP needs to be buffered against excessive political considerations and its leadership to be allowed to function without undue pressure. Also the programme needs to transition from relying excessively on leaders and champions to establish a more solid institutional set-up that can weather political transitions.

An important way of buffering BISP or any other social protection system against unnecessary political pressures is to devise an effective monitoring and evaluation system. Without a monitoring and evaluation system, policymakers, financing agencies and the general public will not know if the programme is operating effectively and efficiently. As indicated earlier, BISP does have a functioning monitoring and evaluation system, but there are allegations that the current monitoring system is too centralized and ineffective.

An effective monitoring system requires a strategic focus and political support more than it requires costly investments in information technology (Grosh et al, 2008). They entail adequate skills, management attention, and funding. Monitoring makes available information on how much money is spent, how many beneficiaries the programme is reaching, and how efficiently the programme is serving them. The monitoring information includes indicators that are compared with targets to assess whether the programme is on track. Managers use this information to adjust and improve the programme.

Programme evaluation addresses the external assessment of programme effectiveness that uses methods to judge whether a programme meets some standards, estimates its net results and impact, and identifies whether the benefits that the programme generates outweigh the costs to society. The most frequently used types of evaluation in safety net programmes are process evaluation, assessment of targeting accuracy, and impact evaluation. Unlike monitoring, programme evaluations are often one-time exercises aimed at addressing a few questions about programme implementation, targeting accuracy, and/or impact.

Thought should also be given to bringing the federal and provincial governments as partners in the evolving devolution of power to the provinces in the context of the 18th Amendment of the Constitution, approved in 2010. To achieve this objective, policymakers will need to ensure consistency between the federal and provincial expectations in the social protection framework and to harmonize systems for design and delivery of social protection within that framework. Currently, the federal and provincial governments share no understanding of their joint roles in policy, design, implementation, and financing of social protection. This is especially relevant because social protection does not figure explicitly in the constitution. Under a decentralized social protection framework, provincial governments may consider establishing their

---

Box 6.1: Federal and Provincial Responsibilities in Brazil's Social Program System

Brazil's Bolsa Familia Program, an education and health conditional cash transfer programme, and the largest programme of its type among developing countries, is a good example of a social protection programme that is managed and implemented in a decentralized manner.

The programme is managed at the federal level by the Ministry of Social Development and implemented by several agencies at all levels of government. More than 5,500 independent municipalities play various roles in implementing the programme, including co-financing, registering potential beneficiaries, monitoring education and health conditions, and prioritizing programme beneficiaries for other complementary services.

A performance-based management mechanism has been developed under the programme to provide incentive for better quality programme implementation at the national level.

Source: Lindert et al. (2007).

---

own social protection authorities to liaise with their federal counterpart. There are good examples of international experience of how different levels of government can work in a coordinated and effective fashion (see Box 6.1).

There is also a need for a better link with beneficiaries. Currently, power rests at headquarters in Islamabad, and communication with beneficiaries is weak. For example, some 800,000 individuals are eligible for transfers but have not received funds. BISP is apprehensive about whether these individuals exist; they have migrated or they are hesitant to receive government support due to cultural reasons.[5] Recent surveys have indicated that there are high inclusion and exclusion errors, with deserving households left out and others included when they should not be. There is, therefore, need for better communication with beneficiaries, better vigilance, and a more decentralized framework.

One concern would be an excessively fast expansion of BISP into many areas. It is important that the programme remains focused on what is already being done, the old advice to 'stick to the knitting'. Involvement in health (*Waseela-e-Sehat*), education (*Waseela-e-Taleem*), microfinance (*Waseela-e-Haq*), and vocational & technical training (*Waseela-e-Rozgar*) should be retained on a pilot basis. Only when resources—financial and human—are available should BISP expand into those areas.

A programme that focuses on eradicating poverty by its very nature needs a long time to achieve its objectives. It will, therefore, be advisable to manage expectations and be more cautious about planned outcomes.

Another area for improvement is the institutional capacity for effective social protection in response to disasters. Pakistan is vulnerable to the ravages of earthquakes, floods, and ongoing conflict-related violence. There have been positive experiences in providing social protection through cash transfers to those affected by disasters. However, institutional capacity needs to be built to provide timely early recovery support in the future at all levels, from the federal government down to the districts.

Finally, it is very likely that the costs of BISP will rise over time to meet even the minimum commitments under the programme. In addition to the costs underlying the implementation of the national safety net, attention will need to be given to maintaining the purchasing power of benefits, which continue to be eroded by inflation over time. Financing such expenditures would be unsustainable in the absence of a larger fiscal space. One option to allow the needed finance would be to reduce untargeted subsidies. Untargeted subsidies to electricity consumers alone have risen to over PKR300 billion annually—nearly 2 per cent of GDP and over six times the most ambitious outlays for BISP (Gazdar 2013). In addition to electricity subsidies, other untargeted subsidies include those provided to foodstuffs such as sugar, which are provided periodically in the face of populist pressures and judicial interventions. There is successful experience in countries such as Indonesia, where untargeted subsidies were phased out and replaced by transfers to the poorest 40 per cent of the population. This would be a good model for Pakistan.

To conclude, BISP has done a commendable job in fulfilling its objectives of providing a countrywide targeted social protection system. It has survived the uncertainty caused by the change in government in 2013, and it has emerged stronger in the process. Indications are that the current PML-N government is supporting the objectives and financial requirements of the programme. Looking ahead, the key issues for BISP will be how its financial sustainability is assured; how it will evolve to conform to the exigencies of the 18th Amendment of the Constitution (i.e. the devolution of power); how successful it is in remaining focused on what it is already doing, without venturing too far into the education, health and microfinance areas, except on a pilot basis and until adequate funding is assured for these programmes; and how BISP improves the linkages with beneficiaries through greater delegation to provincial and tehsil offices.

7

National Database
and Registration Authority

INTRODUCTION

The National Database and Registration Authority (NADRA) is an excellent case study of a successful agency thriving in an otherwise difficult Pakistani institutional environment. In existence for only about sixteen years, it has established credibility for itself not only domestically but also abroad. It is the largest IT company in Pakistan and employs a labour force of about 18,000 mostly skilled employees in eleven domestic and five international offices. It maintains one of the largest multi-biometric identity management database systems in the world and is recognized as one of the top systems integrators of electronic passport technology. The agency prides itself in producing the world's first machine-readable multi-biometric electronic passport. Its database comprises of identity information of roughly 90 million Pakistani citizens, assisted by modern facial and fingerprint identification technologies. The volume of this database stands at a remarkable figure of about 100 terabytes, each passing day increasing by additional data on 30,000 citizens.

This chapter aims at understanding the success of NADRA and examining the factors behind its achievements in the course of a relatively short span of time. It also summarizes some of the remaining challenges for sustained performance that need to be surmounted by the agency.

BACKGROUND

NADRA is an autonomously run and constitutionally established public agency in Pakistan. Its primary function is to run and maintain government databases and statistically manage the sensitive registration database of all Pakistani citizens and Pakistani-origin individuals inside and outside the country. It is responsible for issuing national identity cards to these individuals, securing and keeping up-to-date their sensitive personal information, and ensuring that the identities of these individuals are not compromised by identity thieves. Today, NADRA holds the privilege of being one of the largest multi-biometric identity management systems in the world.

This institution was established in 1998 as the National Database Organization, attached to the Ministry of Interior. Later, in March 2000, the National Database Organization and the Directorate General of Registration were merged to form one entity: NADRA. The mission statement in the NADRA ordinance of 2000 was as follows:

> To introduce new, improved and modernized systems of registration, databases and data warehousing for the country with their multiple beneficial uses and applications in order

to achieve effective and efficient running of the affairs of the State and the general public.

In 2006, NADRA's mission statement was revised to include its commercial aspect. The establishment of National Swift Registration Centres (NSRCs) and Mobile Registration Vehicles (MRVs) enabled NADRA to undertake large-scale public sector projects. Prior to this, in 2003, NADRA Technologies Limited (NTL) was founded as a wholly owned subsidiary to develop customized solutions for the private and public sectors. Today, NADRA and NTL jointly undertake projects with the objective of implementing solutions to bring transparency in businesses and private and public transactions. It facilitates informed decision making for organizations through products such as Verisys, Access Control Systems and Services, and Billing and Collection Systems. The mission statement was accordingly revised in 2006 as follows:

> To create and maintain a secure, authentic and dynamic database that comprehensively covers the demographic, geographic, social and statistical aspects of the citizens of Pakistan, and provide to our own and foreign governments effective homeland security solutions and assistance in good governance. We shall develop ourselves as a "Learning Organisation" in a culture that fosters creativity, innovation, commitment, dedication, continuous improvement and a desire to excel by its employees.

Prior to the establishment of NADRA, data collection was handled manually, resulting in inefficiency and inaccuracy.

The registration did not have an auditing system, and the volume-based incentives resulted in a high risk of faulty data entries by the agents. In view of this, in 2001, NADRA decided to change its business model and introduced double entry operators at random. In case of inconsistency between the operators, the query is moved to a third operator for the final data entry. This ensured the quality of data entered. Through the establishment of NSRCs throughout the country, the concept of a 'live, interactive data entry' was introduced. This helped the largely uneducated population of Pakistan, while simultaneously improving the quality of data entered. MRVs complemented this effort for applicants in remote rural areas of the country.

Another important development in the institution was the renewed focus on in-house competence development.[1] Previously, NADRA had outsourced important functions such as data warehousing and project management and networking, along with support functions of finance and accounts. Moreover, there was an absence of focus on software development or software integration. This was changed with the leadership change in 2001, and the strengthening of the relevant human resources, as well as improvement of the working environment, making NADRA the most computer literate public service entity in Pakistan.

E-Sahulat is the latest product contributing to e-governance. Its success has led to its being used by all electricity distribution companies of the Water and Power Development Authority (WAPDA), Karachi Electric

Supply Company (KESC), Sui Gas Companies, and telecom operators. Moreover, most water and sanitation boards are using the services of *E-Sahulat* in collecting their utility bills from customers. Its simple mode of operation, easy terms and conditions for franchising, and its competitive cost of operation combined with a favourable formula of sharing the dividends with franchisees are some of the factors explaining its successful expansion.

The use of online transactions has had important effects on society. It has helped in changing the bill payment culture of the general public by reducing corrupt middlemen collectors. This has speeded up the bill-collection process in the country. Reduced traffic at banks and utility companies' financial account offices and the possibility of paying bills during off-hours are added benefits. Moreover, irrespective of the locations of utility companies, customers can pay their utility bills from anywhere in the country. Finally, *E-Sahulat* enables online reconciliation of all transactions, providing dispute resolution if needed.

In the face of the perpetually precarious budgetary situation of the country, NADRA has successfully managed to become a financially self-reliant entity that survives off its own operating revenues. Also, thanks to the establishment of the NSRCs, the need for citizens to deal with agents who accept bribes and engage in corruption has been reduced. There is a reliable system of auditing NADRA's staff to track revenue collection.

Given the crucial role of worker remittances in the balance of payments and the overall economy of Pakistan (amounting to about USD16 billion in 2015), NADRA's launch of the National Cash Remittance Programme has proved to be invaluable. NADRA-issued smart identity cards have enabled holders not just to have means of identification but also to receive entitlements in a simpler fashion. The programme was launched in 2012 in collaboration with H&H Exchange Company. The successful deployment of this programme has enabled Pakistani citizens to receive funds safely, easily, and in a timely manner. Those expecting remitted money are able to go to pre-designated NADRA outlets to receive the money transfer, following the confirmation of identity through the customer's identification card.

It is a reflection of NADRA's success that it has been able to outbid technology giants such as IBM, Microsoft, and Sagem for international projects such as the Bangladesh Driver License Project and South African ID Project, among others. Notably, NADRA outbid some of the strongest companies in the international homeland sector in a challenging competition to secure the contract for supply, installation, and commissioning of the Passport Issuing System in Kenya. This firmly established NADRA as a major player in the international homeland security sector.

Table 7.1 summarizes NADRA's key domestic and international clients and partners.

Factors Behind the Success of NADRA[2]

As indicated above, NADRA is a successful institution, thriving not only in its domestic activities but also international projects. This outcome has been made possible by a series of factors, summarized below.

1. **Clear and unequivocal mission statement**: Experience with the performance of organizations indicates that those with clear and specific vision statements and focus are more likely to achieve their objectives.[3] Entities that are burdened with multiple and conflicting objectives are hampered in attaining their goals. NADRA's mission, as laid out in the 2000 ordinance establishing it and also in the revised vision statement of 2006, is very clear, specific, and achievable. It is not burdened with peripheral objectives that would detract it from achieving its core objectives.

2. **Adaptability and seamless evolution:** An important factor of success of institutions is their ability to adjust to existing and evolving challenges and opportunities. Institutions that fail to adapt to the prevailing environment are generally doomed to failure. NADRA has exhibited a remarkable ability to adjust to, and take advantage of, evolving circumstances. As indicated earlier, a year after its establishment, it transformed the business model of registration based on manual data collection, followed by single data entry for automation.

To ensure the integrity of the data, this was replaced by double entry of data. Second, to achieve greater financial autonomy in the face of perpetual fiscal constraints of the public sector, the agency decided to develop lucrative, value-adding, in-house capabilities in areas such as data warehousing, project management, networking and other areas which had hitherto been outsourced. Software development and integration was also undertaken within the agency. Given the increasing focus on transparency, MIS applications were developed to increase visibility into all business functions. Moreover, technology facilitated more rapid processing time and greater reliability, helping achieve the more ambitious financial goals. In the case of the multi-biometric passport, the agency was venturing into uncharted territory. The entire technology was developed in-house. The organization took a calculated risk and succeeded. All this necessitated the hiring of high-end technical human resources for in-house software development, establishment of a proper human resources department, revamping of the office working environment (open floor plans, etc.), flexible office hours for technical staff, flatter organizations and more participative management styles. All this led to a massive change in the business model and enhanced performance.

3. **Attention to customer care and learning:** While there are occasional complaints about the quality of NADRA's service, it has placed heavy reliance on customer care and responsiveness. It developed interactive data entry to eliminate

Table 7.1: NADRA's Domestic and
Foreign Clients and Partners

Clients	Projects
Local Clients	
Ministry of Interior	National Identity Card System
Directorate General of Immigration and Passports	Multi-Biometric Card System
National Highways Authority	E-toll System
Benazir Income Support Programme	MNA/MPA/Senator Forms Processing Project; Emergency Relief for IDPs Project; Smartcard Project; World Bank Scorecard Survey Project
Earthquake Reconstruction and Rehabilitation Centre	Earthquake Reconstruction and Rehabilitation Project
UNHCR, Pakistan	Registration of Afghan Refugees
International Clients	
Government of Sudan	Civil Registration Project
Government of Kenya	Passport Issuing System
Government of Bangladesh	High Security Driver's License
Government of Nigeria	National Identity Management System
Government of Sri Lanka	National Identity Card Project
Corporate Clients	
Telecom	Mobilink; Ufone; Telenor
Financial Institutions	Barclays; Royal Bank of Scotland; Standard Chartered
Utility Companies	PTCL; IESCO; SNGPL; SSGPL

Source: NADRA.

the need for filling manual forms. It eliminated the
need for presenting ID documents and facilitated
a one-window operation by enabling customers
to simply walk in and get registered. It devised
a token system for queuing to serve customers
on a first-come, first-served basis. It established
standard processing and delivery times, which
are generally observed. To handle complaints
and provide customer service, it established a call
centre. All these measures have led to a cultural
change toward customer service. Additionally,
it became a learning organization driven by the
demands of customers, local as well as international.

4. **Relatively young and competent staff:** The
success of any organization depends largely on the
competence and dedication of its staff. NADRA has
been blessed with an effective workforce, which is
young,[4] dynamic, non-bureaucratic, entrepreneurial,
and sees change as a perpetual fact of life at the
workplace. There is a constant endeavour to improve
upon products, processes, and technology. Staff
work under overall long-term objectives, but are
also devising short-term solutions and firefighting
on a day-to-day basis. NADRA also has the most
computer-literate workforce in the country. It has
competitive compensations and benefits, especially
for the technical employees who are compensated at
prevailing market rates, which are much higher than
those for operational workers.

5. **Leadership and management style:** NADRA's top leadership has been strong and involved. The leader of the organization cuts across hierarchical boundaries and obtains feedback directly from the middle management and technical resources in a participative manner. What makes NADRA unique is its ability to balance a democratic culture with an autocratic one. Once decisions are taken on the broad objectives and standards, technical staff is given leeway to perform their functions. On the other hand, NADRA also has retired senior military officials in its management who follow a more hierarchical structure and approach. As a result, for some departments, power distances are high, the approach is more collectivist, and risk-taking is lower. On the other hand, other departments exhibit participative styles of management and are marked by flatter organization. The point is that these two management styles abide side by side under the overall leadership of the chairman.

6. **Entrepreneurial and risk-taking spirit:** A more commercial, proactive, and business-oriented approach pervades in the technical and management portions of NADRA. Risk-taking is encouraged. In many ways, these parts of the organization perform as if they were in the private sector in terms of the entrepreneurial spirit. At the same time, the control systems are very tight and help in bringing visibility and transparency into processes and procedures.

In short, NADRA is a unique organization with a clear mandate and long-term objectives within which a great deal of delegation is provided to technical staff within a very participative environment. Effective controls and performance standards help ensure that the objectives are met and exceeded. Moreover, the need for NADRA to relieve itself from the financial pressures of the government's fiscal situation have helped it to be proactive in successfully seeking domestic and foreign contracts.

REMAINING CHALLENGES

NADRA has become a significant player in the application of identification systems and technology to selected development areas. In addition to supporting critically important applications of biometric technology, social protection programmes, disaster relief projects, and financial inclusion schemes for the economically handicapped, it has also played a vital socio-economic role in bringing into the fold traditionally under-registered communities such as women, tribal groups, and transgender populations. It has also successfully won international contracts for its services. In the process, it has facilitated the enforcement of transparency in many facets of life in areas where the state and the citizenry interact. However, the agency faces some challenges, the resolution of which will determine the sustainability of the success of NADRA.

One such challenge is of institutionalizing its operations, processes, and procedures. The organization has expanded rapidly, employing close to 18,000 staff in 800 fixed and mobile offices. This expansion has not been accompanied by staff training and capacity building, resulting in some erosion of skills. At the same time, the organization has been too dominated by the 'founder's syndrome', with the fortunes of the organization too closely linked to those of the chairman. What is missing is the institutionalization of the operations on a systemic basis to ensure sustainability of achievements beyond the tenure of the leadership. Fortunately for NADRA, the second-tier management (directors general) has witnessed more stability of tenure, which has helped with institutional memory.

A related challenge is the politicization of leadership. There is a fine line between the ability to steer an organization through rough political waters and the need to avoid succumbing to political partisanship. In the aftermath of the 2013 general elections and allegations of possible irregularities, this fine line was crossed by certain statements of the previous chairman.

A third issue relates to the organization's financial situation. During the Pakistan Peoples Party's government, the organization received important financial inflows from the Benazir Income Support Programme (BISP), and UN agencies. However, these are not core services, which can improve the financial sustainability of NADRA. Moreover, while the organization made an earlier start than its international competitors, the latter are now catching up in bidding for lucrative international contracts. Since 2005, there has been no financial support from the federal government, and the rising expenditures have started to eat into the profit margin.

Finally, one of the strengths of NADRA has been the application of a sliding scale salary structure that was more favourable than the government pay scale. With the 'regularization' of NADRA employees, some 95 per cent of the staff have been placed in the government pay scale. This has resulted in a sizeable decrease in the salaries of employees, especially of the technical staff of NADRA for whom there are available options of more favourable employment outside of the organization and the country.

Addressing these challenges by NADRA and the government will determine the success of NADRA going forward. On its part, the leadership of NADRA must strictly refrain from getting entangled in political matters.

8

Punjab Education Foundation

INTRODUCTION

The last twenty years have seen an unprecedented increase in the number of private sector schools across Pakistan in response to the growing demand for education.[1] On the surface this mushroom growth of the private sector in education seems to be a positive development and can be viewed as complementing the overstretched resources of the public sector. However, it can also be viewed as being indicative of a public sector exhibiting a systemic and secular decline in both quality and quantity of education provision across the country. The country-wide low enrolment rates at the primary and secondary level and the high rate of illiteracy in comparison to countries with similar income per capita are indicators of the extent of the crisis in education.[2] This problem is further compounded by the lack of regulation of private schools and deteriorating standards in public schools resulting in large variations in terms of quality and type of education imparted. The differentials in access to good-quality education are found across income groups, gender, regions/provinces, and between rural and urban areas in the country.

There are a number of reasons for the failure of the state in the provision of basic education for all, but arguably the most important is the lack of resources allocated by successive governments to the education sector. Over the past six decades, the average allocation to education, which is now a provincial subject, has not been more than 2.1 per cent of the national GDP. This is indeed very low in comparison to developing countries and neighbouring economies such as Bangladesh and India which spend 2.6 per cent and 3.3 per cent of GDP respectively on education. This consistently meager budgetary provision in the presence of unabated population pressure has stifled growth and impeded improvements in the quality of education from primary to tertiary level.

In the context of chronic resource constraints and the inefficiencies which beset the public sector in developing countries, Public Private Partnership (PPP) is viewed as a potential solution. Partnering with the private sector is thought to galvanize much needed financial resources and also bring in greater functional efficiency otherwise absent in the public sector. Thus, at the World Economic Forum in 2004, more than fifty participating states, including Pakistan, actively proposed the promotion of Public Private Partnership in education provision for overcoming pervasive supply-side bottlenecks (Datta, 2009).

In response to the crisis in education and in line with the prevailing consensus in global developmental circles, the Pakistani government sought to revamp the Punjab Education Foundation (as well as the education foundations for the other three provinces) after 2001. This entailed allowing the provincial foundations greater leverage to realign their objectives and devise innovative strategies to engage the private, profit, and not-for-profit sectors. The provincial education foundations were originally established in the early 1990s as quasi-public institutions associated with the Ministry of Education to promote private sector involvement in education. Since their inception, each foundation has been entitled to government funds with the view that these would be supplemented by resources from international donor agencies, state and federal government grants, as well as voluntary investments.[3]

The Punjab Education Foundation (PEF) is financed by the Government of Punjab as part of its Annual Development Programme (ADP). The foundation fund for the institution was set up in 1991 under the Punjab Education Act. The PEF budget is augmented by various other grants made by the federal government, institutional investments, as well as donations received from international agencies. Ever since the foundation's restructuring in 2005 (as part of the World Bank's scheme of public-private partnerships), its budgetary allocation has grown remarkably.[4] The main impetus for widespread education sector restructuring came with the World Bank assistance of USD300 million for the Punjab Education Sector Reform programme in 2005. Since then the foundation's resources have steadily grown, with the PEF annual budget increasing from PKR400 million in 2005 to PKR8.4 billion in 2013–14. There has been significant and consistent monetary and technical assistance to PEF from the World Bank, Asian Development Bank, and UK's DFID which has been channeled through the Government of Punjab (PEF Annual Report, 2014).

Under the restructuring scheme, the PEF has actively sought to engage the private sector to stimulate growth and improve educational service provision. PEF works in line with the prevalent thinking at the World Bank that the government has the obligation to fund education for all youth, but it need not provide universal coverage since state financing of the private sector is a more cost-effective and efficient alternative to direct provision. Thus, the most commonly advanced justification for PPP is the state's limited capacity to meet the demand challenge, and private sector provision is seen as a means of diminishing the government's burden in expanding the number of schools (Datta, 2009).

However, there is debate over what form PPP can take, with little consensus on the best method to link the public, private, and non-profit sectors in the distribution of public services. There remains a degree of ambiguity on questions such as what type of service, subsidiary or central, the state should retain and what it should concede to the private sector partner (Datta, 2009).[5] In such circumstances, the PEF has adopted a relatively simple model of PPP that has revolved around the initiation and expansion of a handful of well-defined programmes.

PROGRAMMES, MANAGEMENT, AND EVALUATION

The two primary PPP initiatives of the PEF are its Foundation Assisted Schools (FAS) and Education Voucher Scheme (EVS). The other significant and more recent initiatives are The New School Program (NSP) and the Continuous Professional Development Program (CPDP). Under these schemes there are now a total 3,967 partner schools with an enrolment of almost 1.6 million students across all the districts of Punjab (PEF, Annual Report, 2014). The following is a brief description of these programmes.

1. Foundation Assisted Schools

- The flagship programme for PEF is the Foundation Assisted Schools (FAS) which takes an 83 per cent share of the total programme expenditure. The FAS programme aims to further the availability and quality of education through financial grants (subsidies) to private schools of a minimum of PKR450 per child, per month at the primary level which goes up to PKR1000 per child at the higher secondary level. The scheme started in 2005 in six districts with 42 schools and 24,000 children enrolled. In 2014 there were 2,311 schools and almost 1.3 million children enrolled across all the 36 districts of Punjab (PEF, Annual Report, 2014).

- Schools initiated into the programme need to fulfil a variety of criteria, including school location, physical infrastructure availability, teacher-student ratio, and quality of service. Quality Assurance Tests (QATs) are conducted regularly to monitor school performance. A precondition for partnership continuation is the requirement for 75 per cent of the students in the partner school to post a minimum score of 40 per cent in the QAT. Based on their performance the schools are categorized into six grades. According to the latest PEF annual report, 11.7 per cent of the schools under the FAS programme have been classified as grade A, while 6.8 per cent have been assigned a grade D. The majority of schools, around 61 per cent, fall into the B and C category. According to the Managing Director of PEF, there is a large variation in school quality across the province, particularly noticeable between north and south Punjab and between rural and urban areas. Therefore a major challenge facing PEF is to minimize these differentials so as to ensure greater uniformity in education provision across the province.

- The foundation has plans to make school grading publicly available so that the choice or selection of a school is based on reliable information on school quality. It is expected that information on a school's quality would subsequently impact student enrolment which would in turn incentivize school management to work towards improving quality across the different parameters set by PEF. Currently enrolment caps of FAS schools are set by PEF and are only allowed to increase on the basis of a school's performance.

There are, however, limitations on the degree of regulation PEF can impose on FAS schools, given that these schools are privately owned and managed. For example, decisions on teacher hiring and remuneration rest solely with the school management. Although this autonomy could lead to variations in teacher quality, regular interventions such as teacher training programmes and quality assessment exercises are mechanisms to minimize such differences. Incentives such as school and student honoraria given to top QAT performers are also quality enhancement mechanisms employed by PEF.[6]

2. Targeted Educational Voucher Scheme (EVS)

The Targeted Educational Voucher Scheme (EVS) has become a popular intervention in reformative educational initiatives in many developing countries, including Pakistan. Essentially, the scheme aims at enhancing the educational opportunities of poor households, thereby reducing the existing inequity in access to education prevalent in developing nations. Contemporary work on public choice theory makes a strong argument for a voucher system of funding education for the underprivileged. The government subsidizes education through vouchers made available to the poor so that they are able to choose between private schools. Competition from private schools is also thought to enhance the quality of public school education (Datta, 2009).

The EVS scheme was launched in 2006 and involves distributing non-redeemable vouchers worth PKR300 per month per student to parents, enabling poor households to pay their children's tuition fees at participant or accredited private and NGO-run schools. The scheme is distinct from other educational initiatives, as it gives poor households the option to enrol in a school of their choice as long as it is approved or empanelled by the PEF.

Until now the foundation has focused its voucher scheme primarily towards marginalized communities living in underprivileged areas and urban slums. In order to minimize administrative costs, eligibility for vouchers is extended to all inhabitants of an area and therefore, all children in a designated locality are entitled to the voucher. For example, in 2006, 10,000 vouchers were disbursed in various urban slums of Lahore, where the scheme was piloted. The EVS intervention in urban slums is particularly beneficial, as the state does not build schools in unauthorized residential areas. For instance, prior to the initiation of the PEF, households across urban slums in Lahore had no possibility of enrolling in public schools and had very limited access to private schools.[7]

For the EVS scheme to be effective, location of schools is of critical importance, since it is possible that public or private schools are at a considerable distance from a targeted locality, entailing prohibitive transportation costs and safety concerns.[8] In less-populated areas, EVS' success depends on its capacity to attract new private schools to these regions or on the availability of transportation to the nearest private school (Shafiq, 2008). According to PEF, its choice of EVS location and targeting is based on household surveys and information provided by local government. Because of internal capacity constraints the identification of target areas and registration of low-income households for the EVS have been done externally. In fact, one of the major challenges faced by PEF has been the identification of deserving households. For this purpose, PEF is now collaborating with the Benazir Income Support Programme (BISP) which has a comprehensive database on poor households (through poverty scorecards) across the Punjab.[9] In spite of these challenges the EVS programme has expanded quite rapidly: Since 2010 the number of vouchers distributed across the target population has increased from 17, 400 to 208,247, and the number of participating schools went up from 153 to 1,038 (PEF Annual Report, 2014).[10]

The effectiveness of the EVS is measured by increased enrolment rates of disadvantaged children, and the provision of quality education in partner or accredited schools. According to the PEF, its external and internal auditing mechanism has consistently verified and insured that these quality benchmarks are met (PEF Annual Report, 2014). The PEF Monitoring and Evaluation cell enforces 'minimum attendance and performance' of students so that the continuation of the voucher scheme depends on meeting the specified minimum standards. Also, participating schools are delisted from the scheme if they fail to satisfy the criteria twice. However, it is essential that schools are not fined if students fail to meet minimum standards, since this could perversely incentivize schools to either eschew entry into the programme or misreport the results of ill-performing EVS students. Similarly, penalizing students who fall short of performance standards, is discriminatory because the poorest are most likely to fail. This is a fundamental pitfall of most EVS schemes, and the foundation will have to streamline its regulatory process to account for such issues so that their programmes generate positive results over a sustained period (Shafiq, 2008).

Additionally, it is crucial that the voucher is appropriately valued so as to meet the direct costs of a typical quality school. In some cases, it may be beneficial to offer partial compensation for forgone child labour earnings. Although child labour compensation does not currently feature on the PEF agenda due to budgetary constraints, it may be incorporated over time as the scheme is further refined and streamlined.

Given the limited PEF budget, the FAS scheme has received preference over EVS mainly because it imposes a smaller administrative burden especially in terms of the extensive data EVS requires for targeting deserving households in the province. However, the EVS has been continued in spite of this because the project places incentives directly with children and their parents for the attainment of quality education. On the other hand, the FAS scheme places incentives directly with schools and leaves it to the school administration to get needier children to enrol. Therefore, on a comparative scale, the

EVS provides for a more targeted intervention within the demarcated population than FAS (Bano, 2008).

3. Additional schemes

The PEF has complemented its two primary educational schemes with the Continuous Professional Development Program (CPDP) geared towards enhancing teaching quality. Teachers in PEF schools are offered various opportunities for ongoing professional development via training workshops and other programmes. This has been a primary focus of the FAS scheme, and in 2013–14, close to 23,880 teachers had reportedly benefitted from the scheme clustered within districts. The PEF training is facilitated by seven training provider organizations which were selected out of a pool of twenty-four such organizations by the relevant PEF committee. The CPDP consists of three different programmes: teacher training for primary and secondary schools, leadership programme for school management and head teachers and a subject-based teacher training programme. These programmes are run at a cluster level to serve schools within a particular vicinity. CPDP also targets distant or remote schools particularly focusing on those which fail in QATs (PEF Annual Report, 2014).

Also under operation is the New Schools Program (NSP) through which PEF attempts to incentivize citizens to establish schools in underprivileged regions where enrolments are very low and illiteracy rates are high. The NSP, started in 2008, focuses on localities where there is an absence of either public or private schools within a 2 km radius. The NSP is very much in line with the current government's Punjab Education Sector Roadmap Programme (PESRP), which aims to increase enrolment rates and literacy across Punjab, particularly in economically deprived areas. Under the scheme, PEF gives an initial funding of PKR450 per child to an education entrepreneur, with the condition that within six months, enrolment should go up to fifty in the new school. Once the school is established, PEF allows a maximum enrolment of 300 students and provides soft loans for expansion of infrastructure and purchase of textbooks, etc. The schools are regularly inspected by the foundation management and are subject to the same evaluation criteria (QATs) as other PEF schools. In the last five years, NSP has shown remarkable growth. In 2010, there were 110 partner schools with a total student enrolment of 15,879. According to the latest report there are now 618 partner schools with a total enrolment of 87,822 students (PEF Annual Report, 2014).

In addition, the PEF operates close to 7,000 non-formal basic schools: a wider project of the Ministry of Education targeted at confronting the problems of inequity in educational access (PEF Annual Report, 2012). These schools, located within communities, have the advantage of proximity and easy access, which would improve female enrolment and hence address one of the major inequities in education. Upon completing this non-formal schooling programme, students sit the state-administered fifth-grade exams subsequent to which they can choose to continue education in a state- or privately-run school.

Management of PEF

The revamped PEF is a self-governing body with a board of directors comprising fifteen members including a chairperson, which retains both executive and financial authority. The board includes prominent technocrats, philanthropists, and educationists along with provincial secretaries as ex-officio members. The board of directors is responsible for long-term policy formulation and strategic planning of the organization and is supposed to serve for a three-year tenure. However, since 2004 there has been little change in the composition of the board—most members have been reappointed and continue well beyond the three-year period.

For the first time in PEF's short history, the current chairperson of the board is a politician of the ruling party. As PEF is in the centre of the province's recent drive to increase enrolment and literacy across Punjab, it is felt that a politician chairing the board would help steer the foundation along the provincial government's education agenda. It is also thought, albeit counter intuitively, that a politician as chairperson would be more effective in confronting political pressures which mostly come in the form of recommendations for school empanelment or for EVS distribution. However, according to the management the most effective insulation from such political pressures continue to be the well-defined processes and procedures for selection of FAS schools and qualifications for the EVS.[11]

Despite being situated at the heart of the provincial government, the PEF board of directors has enjoyed a considerable degree of autonomy. This autonomy has been a crucial factor in ensuring that by and large professional imperatives rather than political expediency drive decision-making within the organization.[12]

The Managing Director (MD) of PEF serves a two-year tenure and is appointed by the board of directors. Although the position is publicly advertised and open to both private and public sector applicants, since 2004 the MD has been a public servant from the District Management Group (DMG). A stated benefit of a public servant heading the organization is that it facilitates collaboration with other government departments and agencies. Unlike other autonomous government agencies and companies, public servants are not 'parked' in the organization to serve as an MD but are allowed to opt for the position.[13] This has led to a self-selection of public servants who have an interest to serve in PEF thus resulting in greater managerial competence, commitment, and better management of the foundation. This fact has been corroborated by some board members and is also evident from the selection of the current MD.

Directly below the board of directors are the finance, executive and programme committees. The administrative departments work under the MD and are composed of finance, operations, human resource, law, IT, and communications. There is further departmental division on the basis of the institution's various academic programmes, including the PEF Foundation Assisted Schools (FAS), Continuous Professional Development Programme, Education Voucher Scheme, New School Programme, and Monitoring and Evaluation and Academic Development Units.[14]

The staff working in these departments is employed through a competitive hiring process and is generally from the private sector. A total of 229 employees work for PEF which spends just 2.53 per cent of its total budgeted expenditures on HR. This is indicative of a lean and efficiently run organization with no evident overstaffing or redundancy in any department. Given the rapid expansion of its programmes across the entire province, PEF now has two regional offices, one in Rawalpindi and the other in Multan. The headquarters of PEF is in Lahore. This decentralization of operations for North and South Punjab is meant to improve programme management, effectiveness, and geographical coverage.

PEF's Monitoring and Evaluation (M&E) System

Of note is the PEF's autonomous monitoring and evaluation (M&E) system, which reports directly to the institution's board of directors. The M&E department conducts regular sample-based assessment of PEF schools and conducts periodic need-based research and surveys on different programmes run by PEF. This information is critical for strategic planning and decision-making by the board of directors. Lately, the M&E department has introduced a digitized monitoring system which gives real time data/information and generates instant reports about PEF schools. This technology intervention is expected to further improve both the efficiency of the organization and the monitoring and assessment of its various programmes. It is largely down to the active role played by the M&E system that the PEF has come to be regarded as a dynamic and evolving institution where policies and practices are informed by evidence-based research.

Under the overarching framework of the foundation's M&E department and the Academic Development Unit, detailed records of various projects outcomes are regularly analyzed and quality checks on the affiliated educational institutions are maintained. One of the main strengths of the PEF has been its focus on continual evaluation of programmes under a two-tier monitoring policy to safeguard against deviations from stipulated goals—a factor that has derailed many a state programme. Where the M&E department oversees the administrative aspect of programme operation, the Academic Development Unit keeps tabs on quality. Programme implementation is preceded by thorough evaluation via the initiation of pilot programmes and less promising ventures have been readily discarded.[15]

Financing model

As mentioned earlier, the PEF is financed by the Government of Punjab as part of its Annual Development Program (ADP). The foundation budget is augmented by various other grants made by the central government, institutional investments, as well as donations received from international agencies. While the diversity in sources of finance affords some measure of financial security to the institution, this apparent multiplicity of channels, nevertheless, has masked the inordinate reliance on a few select international donor agencies over the last decade.

Since its restructuring in 2005, the organization's budget has increased considerably, with significant combined monetary and technical assistance from the World Bank, Asian Development Bank (ADB), Canadian International Development Agency (CIDA), and more recently by DFID.[16] In the year 2012–2013 alone, the Punjab government received an additional USD70 million from the World Bank, with promises of further assistance in the coming years. More recently, PEF has obtained additional funding by DFID of GBP68.6 million as part of the Punjab Education Sector Roadmap Programme (PESRP). This funding, which is until 2018–19, would focus on out of school children and dropped out children in the most economically-deprived regions of the province.

Given the steady inflow of donor funds since restructuring in 2005, liquidity has seldom been an issue. The PEF's budget has more than doubled since 2010, increasing from PKR4 billion in 2010 to PKR8.4 billion in 2014. Of the allocated budget, about 97 per cent is spent on programme expenditures, with reportedly just 3 per cent spent on HR and administrative affairs. The programme budget has consistently been utilized to the fullest with little surplus amount left over at the end of the financial year. All financial affairs of PEF are overseen by the finance committee, which has recently instituted more efficient systems and processes of financial management. The fact that overhead costs of the organization have been consistently kept low and there has been no wastage of programme funds, signals a reasonably high degree of financial efficiency.[17]

While the PEF management has placed significant emphasis on ensuring transparency and yearly audits are conducted by both internal and external auditing agencies of repute (involving three statutory bodies), the high dependency on donor funding could potentially be a threat to the institution's long-term sustainability. Although the World Bank has been vocal in its satisfaction with PEF performance and has made promises of further assistance, the foundation might have some major strategizing to do after donor funding is phased out in 2017 and the repayment period commences. The recent DFID financial aid to PEF till 2018–19, which is tied to continued budgetary support by the Government of Punjab to PEF, has provided a certain degree of financial security to the organization for the near future.

CONCLUSION—REMAINING ISSUES AND FUTURE CHALLENGES

PPPs such as the Punjab Education Foundation are the new consensus in development where the government and the private sector have effectively collaborated with each other to bolster the objectives of a market-led, growth-driven agenda (Kumar, 2008). The PEF is structured around the premise that the state's primary role is that of a coordinator which retains the jurisdiction and clout to enforce laws and regulations facilitating the market and the private sector. This viewpoint has been alluring for a variety of reasons. One is that the provincial educational committee's overall obligations have been converted into distinct tasks, at least a portion of which has been outsourced. Other purported benefits encompass the enhanced scope for flexibility and devolution, reduction in the probability of politically expedient decision-making, and popularization of the idea of beneficiaries as 'stakeholders' (Bano, 2008). In a refreshing deviation from the norm, the PEF board of directors has been composed of highly-trained professionals with considerable experience in the relevant field, and politically-motivated appointments have been minimal. Moreover, the board of directors has been afforded the requisite degree of autonomy to act on its accumulated experience and implement policies that are deemed viable. Adherence to processes and procedures and reliance on evidence, rather than ad hoc politically-motivated decisions, has dictated the general thrust of policy direction. Such a model has offered a viable alternative to the prevailing bureaucratic system and appears less vulnerable to political pressures. To the donor community, the state has showcased the political inclination for reform and evidently guaranteed a favourable investment environment, in tandem with the global administrative agenda.[18]

However, implementation of PPP in Punjab's education sector is at an early stage, and state policy pertaining to regulatory, legislative, and institutional structure is still evolving. There have been shifts in policy direction with every change in government over the past decade and a half. For example, in a major deviation from the educational reforms initiated in 2001, the 2008 Draft National Education Policy put public sector provision of education in the forefront, while PPP was assigned a secondary role as a substitute in areas with poor existing government provision. With the current government the emphasis has gone back to the PPP as a solution to the educational crisis. The strategy to reduce illiteracy and increase school enrolments in the Punjab is being led by PEF through its programmes such as FAS, EVS, and NSP. These programmes are at the centre stage of the educational reform roadmap being funded and sponsored by donor agencies such as DFID. A major challenge for PEF, according to its managing director, is the added responsibility assigned to it by the provincial government, which is to adopt and reform government elementary and secondary schools. The model to be followed is similar to that of CARE Foundation and other NGOs which adopt and rehabilitate public sector schools in the country. The provincial government's current education strategy does not aim to increase the number of government schools in the province, instead it is focused on improving the quality of existing schools by collaborating with the private sector.

However it needs to be realized that the scale and extent of the educational emergency in the country is so large that a requisite policy response cannot be limited to PPP initiatives alone. The state cannot relinquish its responsibility and obligation to provide free education to all children between the ages five and sixteen—a constitutionally enshrined right. Perhaps a central reason for the failure of the state in providing access to quality education is the paucity of funds allocated to the education sector over the past six decades. Hence there is a dire need to reallocate budgetary expenditures so that the share of education is at least 4 per cent of GDP. The PPP's initiatives, therefore, can act as financial leverage in a resource constrained environment and can effectively supplement the state schools but cannot be considered as complete substitutes. Also, it has to be noted that an overemphasis on private provision in the absence of an effective state regulatory mechanism to check school quality can potentially lead to the supply of low quality education to the poor. A number of studies have shown that the poorest of the poor in Pakistan are still dependent on public schools. Thus to ensure equity and intergenerational income mobility it is imperative for the state to increase the provision and improve the quality of public schools across the country.

Notwithstanding the relative success of Punjab Education Foundation, there is recognition of its susceptibility on a number of accounts: asymmetric growth, poor quality of private schools, variation in school quality across regions, and the requirement for better directed or targeted interventions. The crucial test for the organization will be its ability to sustain itself financially and otherwise after DFID and World Bank funding dries up at the end of 2018 and the process of loan repayment commences. Furthermore, gains from education accrue only over the long run and by their very nature, programme interventions in such domains as education are difficult if not impossible to evaluate with much accuracy in the near term.[19]

To date, the PEF has reported substantial increases in enrolment rates, sidestepped large-scale fund misappropriation, and displayed a degree of professionalism uncommon to the regular bureaucratic process. If its success is gauged on these criteria, it has certainly been a relative success in the Pakistani context. Inevitably, concerns linger over issues such as inequitable access, efficiency, and indication of further marginalization of disadvantaged groups.[20]

Although critiques of PPPs prevail across developing and developed countries, any categorical verdict over the efficacy of this approach in the PEF context would, in the current circumstances, be premature. What can be stated unequivocally is that this approach has yielded respectable results that are significant improvements over the abysmal record of the past.

9

The Edhi Foundation

INTRODUCTION

The Edhi Foundation is Pakistan's largest charitable organization that was established by Abdul Sattar Edhi in 1951. The beginnings of this extensive social welfare institution were humble. Edhi began his philanthropic mission by setting up a small dispensary in Mithadar, a Karachi slum neighbourhood. Almost a decade later, he purchased a Hillman pickup truck that was converted into an ambulance, with 'Poor Patient Ambulance' scribbled on either side. According to Edhi, the ambulance, together with a small-scale local newspaper service were effective advertisement tools for his organization in its early years. However, it was the efficient twenty-four hour service provided by the ambulance and the philanthropist's simple lifestyle that established his reputation and gave credibility to this small-scale social welfare initiative. Initially limited to Karachi, especially its low-income areas, the Edhi Foundation was the first private initiative of its kind at a time and place where both public and private social welfare service provision was conspicuously absent. Describing those early years, Edhi says, 'I began at Mithadar and brought back bloated, drowned bodies from the sea. ...

When families forsook them and authorities threw them away, I picked them up and brought them home.' (Edhi and Durrani, 1996).

Edhis' growing reputation as a selfless philanthropist and his organization's performance led to an increasing inflow of donations allowing for a phenomenal expansion in its ambit of services in subsequent decades. During the 1980s and 1990s, the scope of the welfare organization enlarged from an ambulance service to orphanages, morgues and care centres for the old and homeless, with a network of operations spread across the entire country. Today the foundation has 335 centres across the country providing a myriad of social services. Hence it is not an overstatement that Edhi 'deals with birth and death and almost everything in between' (Brummitt, 2010). Driven by a vision of bringing wider social change in the country, Edhi regards the philanthropic institution he has established as a model for the welfare state that, he hopes, one day Pakistan will become.

The welfare services of the foundation are not limited to Pakistan alone—Edhi has provided relief and rescue operations in the recent Nepal earthquake, donated as much as USD200,000 to the victims of Hurricane Katrina and assisted in disaster relief across Asia and the Middle East. The foundation has offices in major western countries such as the United Kingdom, United States, and Australia.

SERVICES PROVIDED

Although the range of services provided by Edhi has increased dramatically over the past few decades, the core activity of Edhi remains the ambulance service. There are a total of 1,800 ambulances operated by the foundation making it the largest ambulance fleet in the country. The service provides 24-hour emergency transportation to the nearest public hospital for a nominal fee of Rs. 200 per 20 kms. However for victims of terrorism, which has plagued the country for the past decade or so, the ambulance service is provided free of charge.

The ambulance service also transports dead bodies to morgues and takes complete responsibility of burial of unclaimed bodies. According to statistics released by the foundation, staff at Edhi morgues across Pakistan handle up to twenty-five cases a day, 50 per cent of which remain unclaimed. This particular service given to the abandoned, unclaimed and unidentified dead citizens of the society has defined the philanthropic mission of Edhi. Neither the state nor any other welfare organization provides this type of service at a comparable scale.

Over the years Edhi foundation has gained a reputation of working on its own and is not known to seek assistance from either the state or any other social welfare organizations. In contrast the Edhi ambulance service does not work in isolation—in their daily operations and emergency response the ambulance stations coordinate activities with the police, hospitals, and other state agencies and also keep the media informed by sharing information on accidents and emergencies. This close coordination helps improve effectiveness in dealing with casualties from terrorist bombings, natural disasters, car accidents, and civil violence round-the-clock all across Pakistan.

As mentioned earlier, Edhi's remarkable personal credibility has helped in mustering the resources which led to the development of the largest network of ambulances in the country—bridging the huge gap left by failing public sector health and emergency service systems. In fact, until very recently, government action on emergency response was far from institutionalized and no NGO had the resources to even partially plug the conspicuous gap in service provision. Edhi's 1800-strong fleet of ambulances was assembled entirely through citizen donations and continues to grow by the day. Introduction of an Air Ambulance Service has been one of the recent additions with two aircraft and one helicopter in the fleet.

Over time, the Edhi fleet has developed the capacity to respond to accidents and emergencies that the state was ill-equipped to handle. For example, a major achievement was the extension of Edhi services into marine rescue. Trained divers, life jackets, and inflatable tubes are made available to watch towers in Karachi. The institution's marine rescue teams, which have twenty-eight rescue boats, provide rescue services in coastal and flood affected areas of the country.[1]

There are 335 Edhi centres across Pakistan which manage and coordinate a host of social welfare services within their designated areas. After the ambulance service, the second most prominent social service provided by Edhi is its network of orphanages and shelters. The twelve Edhi homes, located in all the major cities, provide shelter and sanctuary to underprivileged orphans, the homeless, and the aged. The largest of such homes is the Edhi Village in Karachi, a 65-acre unit nestled behind the northern slums of the city, which houses nearly 300 children and 900 adults. Along with meeting their basic needs, the orphans in Edhi homes are provided free schooling at the premises and the foundation also finances those who wish to pursue higher education. The aim is to equip these children with the education and training required to pursue a normal life outside the confines of the orphanage. After reaching adulthood the residents of the homes can either leave or decide to remain there indefinitely. Some do leave the orphanages for an independent life while others maintain links with Edhi by choosing to work for the foundation of their own volition.

The Edhi foundation also runs dispensaries, clinics, diagnostic centres, maternity homes, rehabilitation centres, and hospitals in the country. It operates marriage bureaus and runs a free-food facility—the Edhi Kitchen—which provides one meal a day at Edhi centres, feeding thousands all over the country. The extent of the organization network and coverage can be gauged by the fact the foundation has centres located after every 50 km on the Grand Trunk (GT) road and on the National Highway till Karachi. According to the management, the aim of the organization is to improve this coverage further by locating centres after every 25 km on the national highway.

A notable addition to the long list of welfare services provided by Edhi has been the child adoption programme known as the 'Edhi *Jhoola* (cradle)'. Allowing for complete anonymity, unwanted infants are left by their biological parent(s) in cradles placed outside Edhi centres. The infants are subsequently flown to the Edhi headquarters in Mithdar, Karachi, where after a proper legal process they are matched with prospective parents for adoption. On average over 250 infants are given for adoption annually. The adoption programme is managed entirely by Bilquis Edhi—the wife of Abdul Sattar Edhi.

The Edhi Foundation has also embarked on a mass literacy programme, whereby basic equipment such as blackboards, chalk, and rugs have been distributed across all of the organization's rural development centres. The initiative draws on the services of local recruits and volunteers to train men, women, and children in basic reading and writing skills. The organization also runs elementary and primary schools in different parts of Karachi and Sindh.

According to the management most of the welfare schemes run by Edhi have been successful with some noted exceptions. For example, the organization a few years ago embarked on an employment scheme called the Edhi Rickshaw, through which unemployed youth were provided CNG rickshaws. The initiative failed because a large percentage of the beneficiaries reneged on their commitment to pay back the cost of the rickshaws.

Although, in general, adequate standards prevail across Edhi's vast network of welfare centres, there are some symptoms of institutional fatigue due to overstretched resources. The administration argues that instances of lapse in service are not indicative of any serious failing but are due to the organizations limited resources to meet a bourgeoning demand for its services. The organization claims that it uses all resources and means at its disposal to serve the needy and the destitute as satisfactorily as it can. This frugality in spending on the 'non-essentials' is evident by the physical condition of some of the Edhi centres which have very basic facilities and are in a general state of disrepair. For example, there is not any air conditioning, proper furnishing nor computers in most of the centre/ circle offices. Perhaps the ambulance service is the only one that has entered the digital age by making use of trackers and computers in ambulance stations. That too has been driven by the need to manage the complex logistics associated with the vast network of emergency services.

Edhi emphasizes that his social work is not an end in itself but only the first of many steps towards resolving deeper social problems, increasing public awareness about societal issues, and building a force that can eventually usher widespread societal and institutional reformation. Given the fact that Pakistan historically has had no properly functioning state welfare system, even partially filling the huge and growing gap left by the state is a formidable challenge for any private organization.

RELIGIOUS AND POLITICAL NON-PARTISANSHIP

Time and again, the Edhi Foundation has faced opposition and criticism from hard-line religious groups for its progressive views on several societal issues, such as the acceptance of newborn babies born out of wedlock. Moreover, sectarian and religious issues have surfaced where matters such as burials are concerned. Although the organization has frequently come under threat from political, sectarian, and ethnic groups, Edhi has categorically maintained that, 'Hindus, Sikhs, Christians, and Muslims are equal before God' (Edhi and Durrani, 1996). The institution's unwavering commitment to transcend all religious, political, and ethnic divisions is the reason why it shuns the formation of ties with any group in particular. The philanthropist has famously stated that, 'My resolve to remain alone was based on my belief that sectarian, linguistic, ethnic, and political divides must not come into conflict with or become competitive with a charity organization' (Edhi and Durrani, 1996). Some view the Edhi Foundation as a crucial substitute for the charitable work undertaken by militant religious groups in Pakistan, some with purported ties to terrorism.

An example of the Edhi Foundation's non-partisan approach is the 1973 floods in Sindh, when offerings of assistance from powerful feudal lords at Naushero Feroze and Moro were politely turned down with the explanation that it was against the organization's principles to work through other groups. Instead, an extensive independent network of dispensaries and vaccination centres was organized all across the province, and the services of hundreds of volunteers and paid workers were enlisted.

Although the Edhi Foundation has maintained its neutrality, provoking criticism from some quarters, the general response from the wider community has been that of approbation. Its apolitical and non-partisan philosophy has allowed the organization into areas of emergency response that have eluded the state and other agencies, especially when viewed in the context of Karachi, a city torn apart by sectarian/ethnic violence and conflict. The institution has been willing to respond to emergencies other actors would be reluctant to provide for fear of retribution or rivalry. About Karachi's testing circumstances Edhi himself said, 'All ills of society, racialism, ethnicity, sectarianism, class, and party politics run rampant here' (Edhi and Durrani, 1996).

Such remarkable determination in the face of formidable challenges has been one of the distinguishing characteristics of the Edhi Foundation, and one of the primary causes behind its success. The country's inefficient and inadequate state social welfare apparatus has thus conceded critical services, which come under state jurisdiction, to Edhi.

MANAGEMENT STRUCTURE

The Edhi Foundation has a centralized management structure with few lines of authority between management and staff. There are ostensibly three tiers to the organizations management structure. The first is the Board of Directors, which essentially constitutes members of Edhi's family—his wife and four children—and Dr Kazmi, a longtime associate of Edhi. Due to Abdul Sattar Edhi's ill health most of the operational and management decisions are now taken by his son Faisal Edhi who is the vice chairman of the Foundation. Under the board of directors are the zonal managers of the eleven geographical zones which cover the entire country. Each zone consists of multiple circles which are run by circle managers.

The circle managers are responsible for the day-to-day administration and interact directly with employees, donors, and beneficiaries. The organization operates zonal offices in all major cities, including Lahore, Karachi, Multan, Islamabad, and Quetta, and the zonal managers are stationed strategically across major districts to manage the foundation's 335 public service centres spread across Pakistan. The ambulance and emergency services are handled directly by the zonal offices and not by the circles. The circle and zonal managers' report directly to Edhi, and beyond their daily operations, exercise limited authority. All the major planning and decisions used to be taken by Abdul Sattar Edhi but now that responsibility has fallen on the Board, in particular on Faisal Edhi, who is the acting chairman.

The organization's permanent staff constitutes relatively low-paid employees who on average have not more than ten or twelve years of schooling. In a country with a high rate of unemployment and a demographic youth bulge, there is no shortage of semi-skilled labour. The downside of course is in terms of quality of staff hired and a high turnover of personnel in the various centres and homes of the foundations. The learning or training required for any position is acquired informally on the job. The organization also inducts volunteers who sometimes augment the permanent staff, however their induction is controlled and managed by the central office in Karachi. The circle or zonal managers do not have any autonomy over the employment of volunteers in the organization which is yet another example of centralized management.

The system of operations and management at Edhi centres remains informal—operating practices are passed on from the old to the new members of staff. There are no defined processes or standardized operating procedures at any level of management. There has been no effort in the past to formalize the systems of operation or to document procedures. The fact that the organization has expanded over the years in size and scope and continues to deliver, instils a belief amongst the staff that Edhi's designed system of operations, albeit centralized, undocumented and informal, is what works and thus should not change.

With his son Faisal Edhi as the vice chairman and other family members as directors, the philanthropist used to sanction all projects personally on a day-to-day basis and retained the final say in all decisions from the most significant to the least. This highly-centralized management strategy is based on Edhi's belief that having one person in the driver's seat prevents degeneration into mission drift[2] and allows for consistency in decision-making. Perhaps the reason behind this peculiar method of management can be gleaned from his statement that, 'The opposition made me hard and impenetrable whereby instead of becoming subdued I became a dictator. This was the instrument that gave me the power to control and eliminate any eventuality that could lead to curtailing or influencing my mission. ... The issues are clear and the solutions simple. ... Whoever disagrees can go'. The philanthropist goes on to explain that his logic rests on an unflinching belief that he was accountable to no one but God. Edhi argues that most volunteers and part-time workers, whose contribution is relatively meagre at best, are not entitled to criticize, highlight weaknesses, and disparage initiatives. He emphasizes that his obsession to 'know all' was borne out of the vulnerability of his various initiatives to derailment before anything was accomplished and the doubts hurled at the sincerity of his vocation from several powerful quarters (including prominent seths, politicians, and others) (Edhi and Durrani, 1996).

FINANCES

The organization does not publish any annual financial statement nor is the middle management privy to the financial details of the organization. This makes it very difficult to assess the financial health of the organization.

The annual operating budget of the organization is reported to be roughly PKR750 million. After meeting the operating expenses, the surplus funds are channelled by Edhi into expansionary programmes, various emergency response endeavours, as well as reserves.

The main source of funding remains donations from Pakistan and overseas. In order to retain complete autonomy over internal operations and citing issues of mistrust, the Edhi Foundation does not accept donations from international bodies and the government. Although this limits the funds available to the organization, the prevailing perception is that ties with the 'corruption-riddled' state and foreign agencies could compromise the organization's credibility with the general public on whose generous donations it singularly relies and thrives. Having voiced his disillusionment with the state authorities time and again, Edhi has categorically maintained that, 'At no time had I thought it possible to work with or through the (corruption-infested) government ... (whose officials stone-heartedly) swished past the wreckage of humanity' (Edhi and Durrani, 1996).

In 2008 for instance, bequests to Edhi-operated charities swelled up to nearly USD5 million. A sizeable proportion of the assistance comes from overseas Pakistanis and local private sector corporations. Within Pakistan, the bulk of assistance comes from high-income areas across major cities and funds are then transferred to poorer localities which have meagre revenue-generating potential. For instance, most of the donations to Edhi come from

Punjab which cross subsidizes operations in other parts of the country, especially Balochistan. The decisions on budgetary allocations to circles and zones and to the various programmes are made by the centre—the board of directors. Calls for donations are regularly made in newspaper and television advertisements, and the organization frequently writes to donors for assistance. The management asserts that in the organization's decades-long history, a shortfall of funds has been a rare occurrence. The cultivation of such dependable and sustained civil society patronage rests squarely on Edhi's credibility, firmly established after years of effective service delivery.

As mentioned before, the Edhi Foundation does not prepare any in-depth financial statements or annual reports. The only report available on their website is essentially a list of services provided by the organization and the number of beneficiaries of these services in a particular year. Donor faith in Edhi has been such that there have been few, if any, calls for greater transparency. Till his illness, Edhi retained a tight personal grip on all financial matters. In his biography, the philanthropist states that, 'If the money is entrusted and declared to me, I have the right to decide its method of dispensation. I will not succumb to pressure created by those who do not give as much to this work as myself. Neither large donors, nor part-time workers qualify for that authority' (Edhi and Durrani, 1996).

The procedure of donations is quite straightforward—all funds (donations) are transferred directly to the Karachi headquarters, and all disbursement decisions are managed from the central office. In a bid to prevent misappropriation of funds, the organization operates a system of multiple payment receipts. Donors in all regions are required to post copies of payment receipts directly to Karachi, so that a system of cross-checks can be maintained. Where donors are dissatisfied with the placement of their contributions, refunds are readily furnished, and Edhi claims to take personal responsibility for any such violation of trust. However, the gaps in transparency have provoked concern from some quarters and the charismatic philanthropist's son concedes that a negligible portion of donations might be siphoned off by the organization's 13,000 employees, who receive a very modest remuneration (Brummitt, 2010). For reasons of institutional sustainability and strategic growth, and with an increasing number of benefactors demanding objective performance reviews and financial transparency, the Edhi foundation may need to review its approach to financial management in the near future

CONCLUSION—REMAINING CHALLENGES

Owing to the extraordinary scale of its operations and Edhi's predilection for a highly-centralized management structure, the organization's management is essentially a cross between a vertical and a horizontal mode of administration. However, such a hybrid model could potentially entail the disadvantages of both management structures with none of their individual merits. Thus the absence of a concrete organizational and management structure renders organizations such as Edhi *more* vulnerable to mission drift. Already, concerns have emerged from some quarters over the relative lack of professionalism and expertise, particularly as the organization has expanded (Brummitt, 2010).

Although Edhi's persistent efforts to revitalize the institution's sense of purpose have in large part prevented such a drift in focus, things could be different after the philanthropist's demise. In the absence of such high-calibre and credible leadership, mission drift could potentially mar the organization's reputation, rupture its culture, and diminish services to the community. Such concerns are all the more significant because institutions such as Edhi engage with a diverse set of stakeholders that is uncommon to ordinary non-profits. The resultant diversity of the numerous stakeholders' expectations and the organization's aspiration to be self-sufficient perhaps further complicates matters. Questions already abound about the foundation's fate after Edhi's demise, and while Edhi asserts that his two daughters and two sons will take command, without him at the helm, donors may not give as generously (Brummitt, 2010). Yet, regardless of such concerns, given its experience, reputation, and stature, the institution is at present well-positioned to overcome such issues to some degree, if it chooses to focus its energies on doing so.

In the future, as the organization endeavours to further improve and enlarge its ambit of service provision, the inadequacy of resources can potentially become a binding constraint. The management concedes that intermittent shortfalls in funds frequently cause some projects to be temporarily aborted. The capacity to draw and retain resources is a central component in the legitimacy and existence of institutions such as Edhi, which thrive on the social capital they have been able to build in the society. Not only do organizations such as Edhi require society's mandate to survive, but once they have that support, they are vulnerable to pressures to conform to societal norms. While Edhi's high-stature leadership has prevented such degeneration, matters may not remain the same given that he is no longer at the helm of affairs. Therefore a more professional, decentralized, and transparent system of organizational and financial management would need to be put in place for the organization to sustain and improve its service in the future.

The success of the Edhi Foundation lies in its quality social service provision over many decades. Edhi has effectively implemented a vision that has garnered wide-ranging societal support and generated public consciousness about a variety of social issues. He has used his acumen and charisma to formulate an inter-organizational web, however informal, that could effectively implement his vision.

Therefore the main challenge Edhi Foundation will face in the future is to transition from a personality-driven and centralized establishment into an institution with a more professional and devolved management structure. Similarly, the financial sustainability and growth of the foundation would crucially depend upon the personal credibility of Edhi being effectively transformed into institutional credibility.

10

Rescue 1122

INTRODUCTION

Established by Dr Rizwan Naseer, an orthopaedic surgeon by profession, Pakistan's premier medical emergency response service, Rescue 1122, evolved quickly from a small-scale Lahore Pilot Project into an institution with operations spread across the Punjab province. The establishment of Rescue 1122 in 2004 was a hard-won victory for a small team of dedicated professionals determined to fill the void in high-quality emergency service provision in Pakistan. Although the formation of the service was in the backdrop of much political reluctance and bureaucratic hurdles, its eventual implementation was because of the initial support and patronage of the then Governor of Punjab, Pervez Elahi. The fact that since then the service has survived successive political regimes is testament to its success as an institution. To date, Rescue 1122's fleet of ambulances has handled over 400,000 victims across Punjab with services ranging from disaster response and road traffic accident management to fire and water rescue.

FORMATIVE CHALLENGES

The idea of an emergency service germinated from a study done by Dr Rizwan Naseer while he was still in medical school. The results of the study were startling: they showed that almost 95 per cent of trauma victims in Lahore were not able to get an ambulance, indicating the severe paucity of emergency services availability. Although both emergency service and disaster management fell under the domain of the Civil Defense Authority (CDA) of Pakistan, years of bureaucratic mismanagement and institutional decay had rendered these public services quite ineffectual.

The initial effort of Dr Naseer was focused on reviving the functions of the CDA, which led to the emergency preparedness and disaster management programme of the government of Punjab. This was followed by the National Emergency Service Reforms formulated in 2001–02, which had the support of the United Nations Development Programme (UNDP) and the Ministry of Interior. The aim was to restructure the organization by integrating and merging fire and emergency services into one department. Unfortunately, the reforms were never implemented partly because of a change in government in 2002, but more so as a consequence of endemic institutional inefficiencies and a complete lack of ownership of the senior bureaucracy. However, the ten years of effort by Dr Naseer did not go to waste, and in 2004, support finally came from the Governor of Punjab, Chaudhry Pervez Elahi, who approved the Punjab Emergency and Ambulance Service Pilot Project.

The pilot operation was limited to the city of Lahore with Dr Naseer as its director general.

In spite of political support, the challenge for Dr Naseer and his team was to ensure a certain degree of insulation and independence from political interference that could potentially impede the establishment and sustainability of quality emergency services in the province. The initial recruitment and training was done at the premises of the Elite Police training academy and the emergency service was started using fourteen refurbished ambulances with six stations strategically located across the city. Each ambulance was tracked through a satellite-based tracking system located in the command and control centre. The strategic location of the stations and the efficiency of operations resulted in an impressive response time of seven minutes, which has been maintained ever since. The team's determination and professionalism bore dividends: the resounding success of the Lahore Pilot Programme in 2004[1] persuaded the Punjab government to sanction the funding of Rescue 1122. The organization was established through an act of legislation which took a year of preparation and was finally approved by Parliament in 2006.

The initial plans to involve Abdul Sattar Edhi's well-established and extensive ambulance network with Rescue 1122 were shelved after it became evident that the Edhi emergency service, notwithstanding its reputation and credibility, fell short of the sought-after standards of Rescue 1122. The important difference between the two services is that Rescue 1122 ambulances and staff are equipped with state-of-the-art life-saving equipment and are trained to provide emergency treatment, while Edhi provides more of a transportation service to the nearest hospital. In addition, the alternative option of involving the Punjab police with the new initiative was also eventually discarded, as it soon became evident that the desired levels of professionalism would only be achieved if a team was selected and trained exclusively for emergency services delivery.

The commitment to maintain world-class standards led to the establishment of the Emergency Services Academy in 2006—the first of its kind in Pakistan. The first batch of trainees was given medical emergency training by Dr Naseer, who still conducts regular training and motivation sessions for the staff. However, since then, specialized trainers and experts train staff in the latest and most effective emergency service competencies. The skills acquired are frequently adapted to meet local requirements and conditions. The four-month-long basic rescue course involves training emergency paramedics to administer 'pre-hospital emergency care to victims of medical emergencies, accidents, and disasters'. The academy was established at a cost of PKR981 million. To date, more than 7,000 rescuers have been trained and the average cost per trainee of PKR19,902 is likely to go down as the programme is scaled up (PEF, website).

GUARDING AGAINST POLITICAL INTERFERENCE

Formulating a strategy that would make the enterprise resilient as well as insulated from subsequent governments' policy shifts was one of the major challenges for the top management at Rescue 1122. To that effect, Rizwan Naseer laid down a detailed set of rules for the organization's structure and management, as well as protocols and procedures for its daily operations. The carefully delineated guidelines and procedural details served to insulate the infant organization from interference over employment decisions and to guard against undue, politically-motivated influence in its general day-to-day operations.

However, the formulation of these rules and protocols, normally a routine business practice, had to be approached with caution. Rescue 1122 had double cause to be careful— because of its high operational costs and dependence on public funding, it needed to placate the ruling political party and public officials so as to survive politically, as well as financially. Thus, a fine balance had to be maintained of keeping the government on its side while creating space for organizational autonomy.

The procedures in place in the human resource department at Rescue 1122 are a good example of institutional rules that insulated the enterprise from the pressures of political patronage and nepotism. The rigorous recruitment requirements[2] succeeded to sift out all but those fittest for the job, and the grueling six-month training period further filtered any ill-suited workers. The very same practices that ensured the institute's independence could very well have offended the powers-that-be upon whom the institute relied for financial and political survival. However, the director general was able to convince those at the helm of provincial affairs that a well-performing and professionally-run public sector enterprise, known for its service, integrity, and work ethic, was a more viable political asset, than a public organization smeared with allegations of corruption and inefficiency. The provincial government demonstrated its confidence in Rescue 1122 by readily conferring the funds required by Rescue 1122 for expansion, as described in the next section.

THE EXPANSION STAGE

From its very inception, the organization had a clear focus on creating internal capacity to better handle the array of technical issues and problems that sprang up, hindering daily operations. Highly-trained engineers were hired to expeditiously iron out technical glitches, ensure smooth service delivery, and minimize reliance on time-consuming, high-cost foreign expert assistance.

The organization's early successes and burgeoning popularity led to calls for expansion, and between 2005 and 2007, a fire brigade and water rescue service were started.[3] The required resources for expansion, about PKR350 million, were sanctioned by a provincial government now convinced about Rescue 1122's socio-economic importance and resultant political viability. Over the last decade, the institution's operations have extended across all the districts of North and South Punjab, and plans are underway for extending its network at the tehsil level (see Table 10.1 for the range of emergency services provided).

A key challenge for the administration during the expansionary phase was the need to ensure that the quality of service delivery—involving a minimum response time of less than seven minutes—was consistent across the board and there was no variation in service quality across districts. During the initial phase, services were extended to Dera Ghazi Khan, Sahiwal, Gujranwala, Sialkot, Murree, and Sargodha, among other districts of Northern Punjab.

More recently, several community enrolment and training programmes have been initiated, and the goal is to enlist over 100,000 volunteers annually to meet the pressures of increasing demand. In another bid to enhance institutional capacity, Rescue 1122 has launched the Community Safety Programme, whereby communities can be trained and equipped to respond to large-scale emergencies and disasters effectively (Rescue 1122 website).

Table 10.1: Type of Emergency Services Provided by Rescue 1122

Rescue Service	<ul><li>Established after the earthquake of 2005</li><li>Main functions include:<ul><li>Urban search and rescue in collapsed structures</li><li>Rescue from deep and confined spaces</li><li>Water rescue</li><li>Animal rescue</li></ul></li></ul>

Fire Service	• Established on pilot basis in Lahore in June 2007 • Established with the support of Strathclyde Fire and Rescue Service of Scotland, which trained the first batch of officers
Community Safety	• The main features of community safety in which Rescue 1122 is involved are the following: • Fire safety and prevention • Road safety • Community emergency response teams • Safety education • Emergency training of citizens • Collaboration with Chamber of Commerce and Industries • Community Action for Disaster Response (CADRE)
Ambulance Service	• Initiated on 14th October 2004 as a pilot project in Lahore • 97 per cent calls are related to ambulance service • Average response time is seven minutes • Main beneficiaries of this service are the victims of road traffic accidents

Source: Rescue 1122.

MANAGEMENT STRUCTURE

In many ways, Rescue 1122's organizational structure and day-to-day management style match those of a private sector enterprise with clear performance indicators and incentives. There is a well-defined hierarchy, and the division-of-labour is distinctly structured around functional specialization.

'Decentralization, specialization, and formalization'—the elements of organizational design widely deemed indispensable for institutional success—are characteristic of Rescue 1122 operations. Overseen by the director general, the heads of the finance, operations, human resource, community training, planning and development, emergency services academy, and law wings complete the top management. This upper tier designates charge to lower-level managers at the district level, who are in turn responsible for supervising technical staff through well-defined chains of command. Each district retains its own management hierarchy, where the district emergency officer oversees a diverse array of operations conducted by station coordinators, computer wireless operators, lead fire rescuers, auto electricians, and specialized vehicle operators among other staff. Such a decentralized management scheme has allowed for the accomplishment of a solid organizational pyramid with efficient mechanisms for accountability and supervision.

The director general's contract requires renewal every three years as per legislative procedures and is subject to a similar level of accountability and performance evaluation as that of the other management. The DG does not interfere in the day-to-day operations of the organization; his role is clearly defined and encompasses planning, monitoring, and capacity building.

Clear and transparent guidelines are in place for hiring and firing staff, and there have been instances of lay-offs when performance levels have dipped below par. The practice of hiring staff on a permanent rather than contractual basis is a relatively recent development. Although the greater job security initially led to some laxity in staff performance, this was quickly dealt with by introducing more rigorous performance measures.

The organization's management-by-objectives strategy, whereby employees set their own objectives, has allowed for a high degree of objectivity in employee performance appraisal uncommon to most public sector institutions. Moreover, this strategy has enhanced employee performance by circumventing the apprehension and dissatisfaction that stem from unclear job expectations. Clarity in job descriptions and the fact that employees know precisely what is required of them results in better planning and target setting, as well as constructive feedback and communication between managers and staff.

The prevailing employee pay scale in Rescue 1122 is similar to that in other government organizations. There is, however, an incentive and reward system, whereby employees are given an annual honorarium and recognition based on performance. The promotion process is also procedurally transparent and based purely on merit.

Although the organization's procedural details are extensive, they are nevertheless easily understood and are indicative of a clarity of vision and objectives. The level of efficiency in service delivery has been achieved in large part due to considerable internal cohesion and dedicated teamwork nurtured by the resourceful leadership of Dr Naseer.

Interestingly, he still retains much of the staff that assisted him with the organization's establishment almost a decade ago.

Furthermore, well-qualified and professional managers have the autonomy to implement their vision, and there is a remarkable receptivity to new ideas at all levels of management. The culture of openness and inclusivity has cultivated a creative work environment. Numerous community development programmes, including emergency medical services training, have been developed at the initiative of enthusiastic staff members who seek to train the province's student population for active community engagement.

The institution has capitalized heavily on the cumulative know-how of experienced staff members, and the notably high employee retention rates have ensured that gains from extensive staff training are preserved. A crucial factor behind Rescue 1122's continuing success and expansion has been the continuity and stability in its top leadership—an anomaly in comparison to the experience of most public sector institutions in the country. Rizwan Naseer has adeptly skirted undue bureaucratic and political interference and made decisions which have been process based and rest on sound analysis and technical knowledge. Where many other public sector institutions have languished under frequently changing and ill-suited leadership drawn from bureaucratic ranks, Rescue 1122 remains an exception.

The high level of commitment and dedication that has become the hallmark of Rescue 1122 operations is a rarity in a public sector organization where rewards do not necessarily align with the degree of efforts made. The persistent need to improvise and operate efficiently has demanded an unprecedented degree of dedication and commitment from the Rescue 1122 staff. The top management has perceived the need for continuous reinvigoration of staff morale in the given environment, and to this end, expert motivational drills are regularly conducted. A factor which has contributed to the high level of motivation and dedication of the employees of the organization is the role Dr Naseer has played as its director general. While delegating management effectively, he has led the organization from the front—volunteering his services by being part of both training and field operations regularly.[4] He periodically conducts motivation sessions with the staff, which have helped develop a culture of dedication and efficiency within the organization.

TECHNOLOGY-AIDED SERVICE AND MANAGEMENT

Rescue 1122 has a state-of-the-art centralized monitoring, tracking, and evaluation system that seeks to ensure uniform quality of service delivery across the province. Through this system, the central control room maintains a steady flow of communication with emergency vehicles and substations. Possible instances of misuse of service or petty corruption are prevented through the presence of a GPS-based fleet-tracking system equipped with a street-level map to assist with effective surveillance and fleet management. The institution's centralized tracking system involves a provincial monitoring cell that works in conjunction with district control rooms installed with external and internal cameras. In addition, an extensive call-monitoring software system is in place. The organization's wireless communications system serves as the backbone of the service due to its indispensable role in effective management of emergencies and disasters.

The state-of-the-art centralized tracking system technology allows the organization to efficiently blend top-down and bottom-up communication with an unabated flow of information across all tiers of the vertical management system. The technology has aided formal procedural operations and allowed for continuous feedback from the 'client' group whilst imposing none of the costs traditionally associated with the laborious and extensive paperwork that is the trademark of state-run institutions.

FINANCES

Although the organization was able to procure funds for expansion from the provincial government, the ever increasing demand for emergency service provision in the province has resulted in overstretched operational resources. The top management has identified several nodes of service delivery that remain understaffed and where working hours are stretched regularly without any overtime pay. A major challenge for the organization has been the government's implicit reluctance to furnish Rescue 1122 with pay increases that are similar with those accorded to other public sector bodies. However, the top management, to some extent, has been able to negotiate successfully with the government in this regard. As a result, monetary incentives and concessions have been provided to ensure the requisite level of dedication and commitment.

In the face of chronic financial pressures, the organization has learnt to survive with a relatively modest budget. According to Dr Naseer, the total budget of Rescue 1122 is equivalent to that of a public hospital such as the Mayo and Jinnah hospitals in Lahore. A key factor which is pointed out behind the operational and financial efficiency of the organization is that emergency service is based on a *response time* model rather than a *population*-based model. The response time model entails maintaining a certain emergency response time, for example, seven minutes, with the given operational capacity and infrastructure. On the other hand, the population-based model would require a certain operational capacity and infrastructure dependent on population size and independent of the response time. According to the MD, the latter model if adopted would have resulted in a much larger infrastructural investment and substantially higher operational costs.

A recent focus of Rescue 1122 is to empower local communities to respond to their own medical emergencies through extensive training programmes that are already underway in many districts. This would allow the organization to cut back on its manpower resources and lay the foundation for community responses to local emergencies. In tune with the administration's commitment to tough budgeting and capacity rationalization—unusual in a public sector enterprise—extensive revenue reports are regularly produced by Rescue 1122.

The institution's focus on indigenous manufacturing and repair has been part of its cost-cutting strategy, where close to PKR2.2 billion in foreign exchange has been saved due to local fabrication of international-standard emergency rescue vehicles and high-rise firefighting platforms. Such cost-cutting endeavours have been important in helping the organization maintain financial viability in the face of budgetary constraints.

In a recent meeting on governance reform in the Punjab government, it was noted that Rescue 1122 has developed a reputation across the province of efficient service delivery in spite of the lack of operational resources. Interestingly, a reason cited for the organization's insularity from local level extortion and patronage networks is not just its credibility and reputation, but also a recognized paucity of any extra funds available to pay off local touts and mafias.

POSITIVE EXTERNALITIES

A reported outcome of the expansion of Rescue 1122 emergency services, into the rural areas and small towns across Punjab, is the noticeable improvement in service delivery at local health units. As the absence of a doctor or nurse on duty at the nearest health unit was reported by Rescue 1122 staff, this consequently led to a fall in absenteeism in some units. Although this evidence is fairly anecdotal, it reflects the positive externality of Rescue 1122 on downstream healthcare facilities. However, the complete absence and poor condition of existing healthcare facilities, especially in rural areas, is the binding constraint under which all emergency services function, limiting the eventual positive impact on the population.

Another interesting impact of Rescue 1122 has been in the form of legislation on motorcycle gangs and one-wheeling. The organization's research wing has extensive data on injuries and deaths caused by one-wheeling, which allowed Dr Naseer to push for provincial-level legislation against both motorcycle gangs and one-wheeling. The implementation and enforcement of the law, however, has been quite intermittent and for short durations.

MANAGING AN EFFECTIVE PUBLIC RELATIONS CAMPAIGN

Over the past ten years, Rescue 1122 has not remained wholly immune to the general scepticism and cynicism levelled at most public sector initiatives, in a country plagued by political contrivance and corruption. Although the voice of cynicism emanated most frequently from a sensationalist media, over the years, the organization's management has learnt to use the media to its advantage. Time and again, television advertisements have been aired to promote Rescue 1122's image as Pakistan's premier emergency services organization with a highly commendable response time of seven minutes.

Managing expert public relations has helped garner initial wide-scale support as well as firmly cement the organization's position and image as a viable and growing institution. Such PR exercises have now been extended towards highlighting the organization's emphasis on community services. The management has been at pains to emphasize that the organization's perceived success or failure relies heavily on how well the public understands its mandate. To facilitate this understanding, much effort continues to be directed at ensuring that the client public accurately perceives Rescue 1122's primary goals and functions.

Conclusion—Remaining Challenges

Rescue 1122's dependence on a charismatic leader and his dedicated team means that the organization has yet to prove to be capable of surviving leadership transition. The director general is mindful of this fact and continues to establish management reform aimed at enhancing institutional resilience.

Those at the helm emphasize that even after a decade of operations, each passing day presents a different set of challenges for the team. What is certain, however, is that without the remarkably dedicated leadership, the organization would struggle to operate at the level of professionalism it currently maintains. In spite of its credibility, the uncertainties from political transition and chronic financial strain have been frequently felt within the institution. The meticulously laid down procedural guidelines and legislative protection have, to a great extent, immunized the organization against the uncertainties ensuing from political transition at the highest level. The organization's relative youth has nevertheless caused considerable uncertainty at each of the three instances of government change since 2004.

According to Dr Naseer, there are three important challenges for the future growth for Rescue 1122. The first is to raise standards to international levels in all areas of service. The second is to undertake evidence-based research which would help formulate organizational strategy. Finally, the organization aims to establish community emergency response teams at the tehsil level. The latter would eventually lead to more sustainable, healthier, and safer communities. A planned initiative in this direction is that of a 'community watch', where community volunteers are trained in emergency services so that they can take responsibility for their neighbourhoods and localities.

Overall, Rescue 1122 stands out as a success story in the midst of a poorly functioning public sector. It has all the attributes of a successful organization: strong leadership but with devolved management and robust operational procedures. It has been able to develop a culture of service delivery and a reputation for efficiency and honesty. The standards of service have been maintained despite growth in operations across districts and a binding financial resource constraint.

11

Shaukat Khanum Memorial Cancer Hospital[1]

Introduction

The Shaukat Khanum Memorial Cancer Hospital and Research Centre (SKMCH & RC) is Pakistan's first specialized cancer treatment unit and one of the largest not-for-profit tertiary healthcare facilities in Pakistan. Established in Lahore in 1994, the hospital not only specializes in the treatment of cancer, but is also a leading centre of cancer research in the country. Spread over a 20-acre area, the hospital has a total staff of 1,800 and provides free diagnostic facilities and treatment under internationally recognized standards and protocols using state-of-the-art equipment.

The Shaukat Khanum Memorial Trust (SKMT) fund was founded by Imran Khan, the cricketer turned politician, in 1989, in memory of his mother who had died of cancer some years earlier. The tragic death of Imran's mother due to cancer along with a realization that the majority of Pakistan's population had no access to any form of diagnostic and treatment facilities for cancer became the driving force behind his ambitious endeavour to set up a cancer hospital.

Supported by a small but dedicated team of friends and doctors, Imran Khan's mission was to establish a research hospital which would dispense world-class cancer treatment on a need-blind basis, train healthcare professionals in the latest medical developments and conduct state-of-the-art cancer research. Hence, the biggest challenge confronting Imran and his team was to raise the required resources for such a hospital. The funds needed to set up a high-quality integrated cancer treatment centre were substantial and the majority of medical experts, whom the team consulted, were sceptical of the project's feasibility and sustainability. At the same time, the design and development of a hospital blueprint to match international standards within the constraints of a developing country was also a formidable challenge. While Imran Khan took the onus of fundraising, his cousin, Dr Nausherwan Burki, was tasked with developing the project blueprint.

It took three years of persistent hard work and a well-designed domestic and international fundraising campaign to raise the requisite amount of USD22 million for the first phase of the project. Imran Khan's celebrity status and popularity played a critical role in the success of the fundraising campaign. The amount raised helped finance the building of the hospital infrastructure and procurement of the diagnostic and treatment equipment. The 20-acre plot of land in Lahore was provided free of cost by the

Punjab government which had sanctioned it for the building of a hospital.

Twenty years on, Shaukat Khanum Hospital is an established name in quality cancer diagnosis and treatment. Almost 75 per cent of the patient visits are financially supported at the hospital which is a remarkable achievement that has been sustained over two decades. The hospital's commitment to remain at par with the latest technological developments in cancer treatment has led to the procurement of Pakistan's first PET-CT scanning system in addition to several ongoing complementary investments that have added to SKMCH & RC's already rich set of cancer treatment equipment.

The hospital now offers post-graduation training programmes in nuclear medicine, radiology, medical oncology, radiation oncology, pathology, medicine and anesthesia. It also has a four-year training programme in internal medicine that is approved by the Fellowship of the College of Physicians and Surgeons of Pakistan (FCPS) as well as the Royal College of Physicians, UK. There is a team of UK and US-trained pathologists and radiologists who provide state-of-the-art diagnostic facilities to cancer patients. Patient referrals come from in-house physician services, as well as from the hospital's numerous collection centres and diagnostic centres that operate nationwide. Shaukat Khanum Hospital is now aiming to expand its reach to other cities across the country—construction work of Pakistan's second Shaukat Khanum Memorial Cancer

Hospital and Research Centre in Peshawar is already underway.

Management: The Shaukat Khanum Hospital has a three-tiered management structure with a nineteen-member board of governors at the top, under which is the CEO, followed by five directors. These directors manage the medical division, nursing division, finance, resource development and operations. The medical, nursing, and operations division have various departments functioning under them.

With the exception of five permanent members on the board of governors, which include Imran Khan, the rest of the members serve a maximum of two terms of five years each. The board's primary role is governance, which entails an oversight of programme delivery ensuring both financial viability and service quality. The board's role is carefully delineated and it does not interfere in the day-to-day running and management of the hospital. The management of the hospital is delegated to the CEO and is further decentralized to each of the divisions and then on to the departments. These departments in turn follow carefully outlined processes, procedures, and protocols with the aim of providing quality cancer care to all patients irrespective of their income profile.

TECHNOLOGY AND INFORMATION-BASED MANAGEMENT

The management of the hospital is aided by a state-of-the-art Management Information Systems (MIS) which facilitates inter- and intra-departmental communication allowing a continuous flow of information across all levels of the management and administrative systems.

Aided by modern technology in an industry where manual records pervade, the institution's extensive electronic database, procedural details and regulatory controls have allowed it to institute quality assurance and accountability mechanisms that have been central in ensuring operational efficiency. Procurement discrepancies, record tampering, misreporting of entries and unauthorized payments are also circumvented through the use of modern tracking systems. The following is a description of the MIS system, which was built in-house, with the patronage of the CEO[2] of the hospital:

> Our MIS system is totally unique and no other hospital is even close to it! The system includes modules for electronic health record, financial record, administrative processes, fundraising, etc. Probably the patient consent form is the only paper work we have otherwise 99.9 per cent of the interaction we have with our patients is on the system. So everything— hire, fire, purchase—is either through e-mail or through the hospital system. It is a complete application which has been developed in-house. The ready-made systems are available in the market but they are too expensive. When we developed our system, at that time in the market an average system was USD5 million and if you go for a good system then it is worth up to USD200 million.

PERFORMANCE BENCHMARKS, PARAMETERS, AND SERVICE EFFICIENCY

In order to ensure quality service provision, each department has its own set of efficiency measures or benchmarks for its staff at both the individual and department level. Some examples of these benchmarks are: percentage of people getting free treatment, delivery of quality care, percentage of on-time reports in the pathology and radiology departments, the cost and the returns of fundraising, the turnover in human resources, etc. The benchmarks set by individual departments are in accordance with prevailing international standards in the healthcare industry. In the absence of a relevant standard, the department is encouraged to come up with its own measure and track it over time. The performance of the departments is shared regularly in the hospital operations meeting. Similarly, on the clinical side, there is an executive board that monitors internationally recognized clinical benchmarks such as infection rates, average length of stay, and readmission after surgery, etc.

The hospital has also applied for a premium external accreditation known as the Joint Commission International. Because of the prevailing security situation in Pakistan, the commission has not been able to visit the hospital. However, the hospital management is confident that it would receive the accreditation without any problem. Besides this, there are several agencies such as Pakistan Centre for Philanthropy and A. F. Ferguson which audit the hospital periodically. The Pakistan Nuclear Regulatory

Authority keeps a check on radiation safety measures and there is an audit for food services also.

EMPLOYEE INCENTIVE MECHANISMS

The hospital has a total strength of around 1,800 employees consisting of consultant staff, residents, nursing staff, and allied medical and support staff.

A key challenge for the hospital administration has been to hire qualified staff in various departments who meet the requisite standards. While efficient service delivery has become the hallmark of the institution, this has been a consequence of a highly selective recruitment strategy. The country's insubstantial investment in training healthcare workers has generated a serious shortfall of nurses, paramedics, laboratory and surgical assistants, management and public health experts and this complicates matters for institutions such as Shaukat Khanum Hospital, which aim to employ well-trained professionals across all levels of operation.

The hiring processes of the HR department are transparent and purely merit-based with no room for any type or form of influence or interference. The management maintains that the prevailing salary structures are competitive, with annual performance based appraisals. In order to incentivize and retain doctors and specialists, the remunerations and annual pay raises are based on the quantity and quality of work done, i.e. research, clinical output, teaching, etc. Moreover, the hospital provides complete health cover/

insurance to all its employees—a major factor behind the claimed high retention rate.

The hospital employs highly qualified UK- and US-trained physicians who draw on a multidisciplinary approach to administer world-class diagnostic, treatment, and support services to cancer patients. The institution has capitalized heavily on the cumulative know-how of experienced staff members and the notably high employee retention rate has ensured that gains from extensive staff training are preserved.

Finally, the hospital encourages regular volunteer participation and short-term internships, where the minimum required qualification is a matriculation degree. The management underscores that the preservation of high quality standards over a prolonged period has been one of the key challenges for the administration and has necessitated an unprecedented degree of professionalism and expertise.

PATIENT SELECTION—BRIDGING THE DEMAND-SUPPLY GAP

As the only hospital in Pakistan specializing in cancer treatment, a key challenge for Shaukat Khanum Hospital has been to cope with the ever-increasing demand for cancer treatment. Although the institution has been on a path of expansion since its inception almost two decades ago (see Figure 1), the supply response has been understandably inadequate in addressing the disproportionate demand-side pressures.

Figure 1

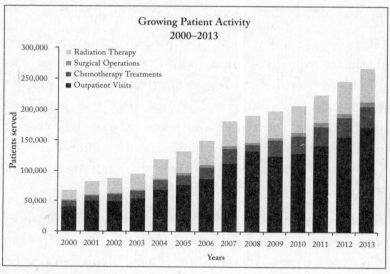

Growing Patient Activity
2000–2013

Source: SKMT Annual Reports.

Figures indicate that close to 150,000 Pakistanis are diagnosed with cancer every year with a mortality rate of over 50 per cent.[3] As the sole provider of specialized cancer treatment in the country, with a comprehensive paraphernalia of cancer diagnostic and treatment facilities under one roof, the hospital is under increasing pressure to respond to the burgeoning needs of the public. However, the hospital's current capacity only permits it to entertain a fraction of these patients. Optimal supply-management has, therefore, been a challenge and the hospital administration has to selectively sift through scores of prospective patients. While this has inevitably caused criticism and discontentment, the hospital management has categorically emphasized that the institution's commitment to world-class quality standards precludes the possibility of compromising quality for quantity. The unequivocal stance has been to retain the cases that can benefit the most from treatment and then provide them with the finest care possible. The following is an excerpt from the interview of the CEO, which details the patient selection procedure:

> Our initial assessment is not monetary; it is rather clinical. We do not ask the question of whether the patient has the ability to pay for the treatment or not. You come to the walk-in clinic and get yourself examined—nobody charges you anything. We just look at the data you have, the paperwork you have and see whether you have cancer or not. If someone is diagnosed with cancer then we see the type and the stage of the cancer. After all this, we decide to admit the patient. For those diagnosed with cancer and not admitted, there can be two reasons. Either the cancer is at such an advanced stage that we cannot cure it or there is a possibility that it can be cured, despite its advanced stage, but we don't have that much capacity to treat it. After you have passed the clinical gate then you tell us whether you can afford the treatment or not. Everybody is given a bill. Those who say that they can't afford the treatment are then referred to the financial support department, and they interview people to see whether the person is eligible for support or not. Generally, we do believe what the patient or his family says. Sometimes, when we have some doubt, we send our inspection team for visits. Though it's small, we do have a field visit team. In cancer there is no emergency case except for a few cancer types. Our target is that patients are given an appointment no later than seven days after they walk into the clinic.

In an attempt to overcome capacity bottlenecks, the hospital has lately initiated a host of expansion programmes. These have involved the extension of facilities across the hospital's main premises in addition to the construction of a brand new unit in Peshawar following a generous land grant. The hospital aims to build a series of chemotherapy delivery units furnished with minimal but essential associated auxiliary facilities in a number of cities. The eventual goal is to extend these into full cancer hospitals. The Peshawar project is part of SKMCH & RC's wider blueprint for the eventual construction of a series of small hospitals in several cities across the country in an attempt to keep up with increasing demand pressures. The establishment of the Shaukat Khanum Diagnostic Centre and Clinic in Karachi in 2007 was also in line with this goal. The overall objective is to scale up the success of the original model all across Pakistan in a relatively low-cost and speedy manner.

FINANCES

In 2012, the hospital's annual budget was PKR5.1 billion. This has been a huge step up from its initial revenue of PKR141 million in 1994. According to the hospital management, 50 per cent of the funds derive from donations (including zakat funds) from both local and overseas Pakistanis (see Figure 2). The remaining amount is acquired through revenues generated from various hospital services. The institution has tapped into a series of innovative strategies to raise funds. These include regular organization of fundraising events/dinners, availability of SMS and landline donation services and reward point schemes that are operated in collaboration with various banks. The aim is to optimize the institution's revenue generating potential by ensuring that Pakistanis from all strata of society have the opportunity to make a contribution. The funding sources are diverse, mitigating to some extent the risk of dependence on a few large donors. The hospital's uncompromising dedication to quality standards and professionalism has been pivotal in garnering the support of key stakeholders and donors.

Surplus amount accumulated at the end of the year is invested by the hospital. An investment committee of the board is responsible for devising investment strategies. In the past, the hospital has invested in real estate, banking instruments, interest-bearing certificates, etc. Zakat funds and revenues from services are not invested.

Similar to other not-for-profit enterprises, a key concern for the administration has been financial management and sustainability. Although the hospital has a significant and dependable high-profile donor base, the main issue is a lack of capacity to meet the constantly increasing demand for treatment. To some extent, rectifying the capacity issue would also help the hospital financially, as the numbers of self-financing patients would consequently increase, while ensuring that 75 per cent of the patient visits continue to be financially supported.

According to the management, 75 per cent of the patients get financial support or subsidy in treatment costs. Thus

Figure 2

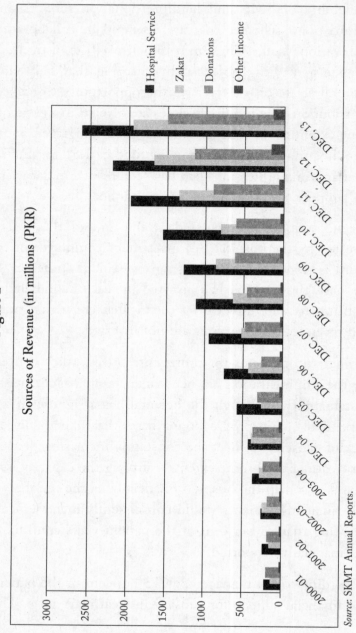

Sources of Revenue (in millions (PKR)

■ Hospital Service
□ Zakat
▨ Donations
■ Other Income

Source: SKMT Annual Reports.

25 per cent pay the full cost of treatment which on average comes to approximately PKR1 million per patient. Among the 75 per cent who are subsidized, a significantly large proportion receives completely free treatment.

While the start-up capital drew entirely from prominent donor contributions, over time donor reliance has been steadily scaled down. The hospital's focus on seeking out innovative ways—such as SMS and landline donation services—to upgrade its revenue base sets it apart from most public sector medical institutes which continue to languish under severe financial and capacity constraints. Moreover, in tune with the administration's commitment to tough budgeting and capacity rationalization, there is regular production of extensive revenue reports.

Conclusion—Remaining Challenges

The most significant challenge facing Shaukat Khanum Hospital is the availability and retention of high quality human resources. In particular, retaining qualified doctors who have an international market is perhaps the most challenging aspect of administration and management.

Another important challenge is electricity supply. The chronic energy shortage in the country has led to frequent and unscheduled power cuts for the past five years. This has come at an enormous cost to the hospital which has to have constantly running backup generator systems. According to the CEO of the hospital:

An average CEO in USA does not have to worry about electricity. Once he has got the connection, he is good to go. All he needs is one back-up generator. And how many do we have to put in the system? Many. In the recent incident of fuel shortage which happened prior to the Long March, we stored 14 days' supply of fuel. These are challenges which someone else might not face elsewhere.

Given the pervasiveness of political wrangling in the country, Imran Khan's foray into politics has sometimes generated unwarranted complications for an institution that has drawn heavily on its founder's widespread popularity. Allegations over the misappropriation of donor money by rival political groups posed a serious threat to the inflow of donations at several points in the institution's history. For instance, PML-N's publicly cited misgivings about Shaukat Khanum Hospital's financial transparency were highly detrimental to donor inflows in 1997 and the hospital has come under increasing scrutiny as Imran Khan's political persona has become more prominent. While the hospital produces detailed financial statements, according to standard accounting procedures on a yearly basis, and makes the information known to the general public in a bid to maintain financial transparency, minimizing the potential damage from negative publicity remains a challenge.[4]

The management concedes that attaining self-sufficiency in finances is a leading objective and challenge. In spite of a steady stream of funds from reliable donors, since the hospital's inception two decades ago, there is recognition that donors can be fickle and represent a limited source of finance at best. Given the fragility of the political and economic situation in the country, the institution's reliance on donations for over half of its total revenues puts its long-term financial sustainability at risk. Moreover, any large-scale expansionary programmes will necessitate funding at a much wider scale than that currently afforded by donor financing. However, as the hospital sets about strengthening its internal revenue base, by capitalizing on its strengths and expanding its network of collection and diagnostic centres, a key pitfall to avoid will be detraction from its ultimate social mission of providing affordable cancer treatment to scores of underprivileged Pakistanis, who have no other avenue for redress.

Finally, the management realizes that the hospital has yet to effectively tap into the marketing potential of its research-based operations. There is an acknowledgement that most people see Shaukat Khanum Hospital merely as a cancer hospital and remain unaware that its operations extend to a full-fledged Research Centre that draws on state-of the-art MIS to conduct clinical as well as basic cancer research. Although Shaukat Khanum has been a leading innovator in Pakistan as far as tapping into donor funding is concerned, the hospital's marketing department admits that its fund-raising potential is yet to be fully exploited.

12

The Story of Failing Institutions

The year was 1955. A new airline had just been established in a relatively new nation. The airline—Pakistan International Airlines—quickly became a regional leader in the airline industry. In 1960, it acquired a Boeing 707, becoming the first Asian airline to own a jet aircraft. In 1962, it broke a world record for the fastest flight between Karachi and London. In 1964, PIA earned the distinction of becoming the first airline from a non-communist country to fly into the People's Republic of China. In the 1980s, PIA helped establish Emirates by leasing it two of its airplanes and providing technical and administrative assistance. In those heady days, it was a matter of great pride for Pakistanis to have such a successful national airline.

Fast forward twenty years, and PIA has become the epitome of a failing organization. It is known for its poor service, long delays, flight cancellations, shortage of planes, unclean toilets, poor management, lack of maintenance, aged fleet, corruption, and financial problems. It cannot compete with the very airlines that it had helped create. During the past 15 years, PIA has posted profits only during 2002–2004. Nearly every year the government bails it out, but even then, there are no signs of improved performance.

Why did PIA's performance and image collapse so spectacularly and tragically? What were the structural factors that nullified its flying start as a successful national carrier?

In the previous nine chapters of this book, we have examined organizations that are considered successful in the pursuit of their objectives despite all odds. In this chapter, we analyse two Pakistani organizations that have failed their customers and their shareholders. PIA is one example. The other is Pakistan Railway.

While these institutions had much going for them, they have faced a series of structural and organizational problems that inhibit their growth and stifle their initiatives. It will be important to isolate these problems so that they can bring into sharper focus the achievements of the successful organizations reviewed in the previous chapters, and thus help us draw lessons for the performance of organizations.

PIA—FROM LEADER TO LOSER

At the basic level, the various problems of PIA are a manifestation of three broad structural and managerial problems. These problems include: political interference in hiring and firing, resulting in massive overstaffing; leadership issues and powerful unions; and poor regulatory arrangements.

- **Political interference in hiring and firing**: In an industry where employee per plane ratio is often used as a key indicator of efficiency, PIA has one of the highest ratios of employees per plane in the world. For the fully operational 31 planes, there are about 19,500 employees, resulting in employee per plane ratio of about 630. The comparable ratio for some other airlines are: Sri Lankan Airlines 281; Thai Airways International 245; Emirates 245; and Turkish Airlines 70. This suggests that PIA is not even half as efficient, in terms of number of employees, compared to other airlines.[1] The airline is also top-heavy, with over 11 directors, 40 general managers and over 300 deputy general managers, costing a large amount in salaries and benefits, and making it difficult to justify the continued government bailouts at the tax payers' expense.

The reason for this dire situation is political interference in the hiring and firing of the employees and senior managers. Even when efforts have been made to lay off workers, they are strongly resisted. An example of political appointments is the Sacked Employees Reinstatement Act of 2010 passed by the Pakistan Peoples Party government, under which employees sacked during the Nawaz Sharif tenure (1997–1999) were reinstated. Since these workers were out of the relevant workforce for over a decade, there was a serious mismatch of skills. Moreover, these reinstated workers were given their positions based on what their seniority would have been if they had continued with the organization. This led to serious tensions with the current employees whose promotions were now at risk due to these lateral entries. In short, overstaffing is a reflection of a much bigger problem of political interference in the human resource management of the organization.

• **Leadership issues and the role of trade unions**: There is a plethora of trade unions associated with PIA, each catering to a specific type of employees, but all exercising an impact on the decision-making of the leadership. Pakistan Airlines Pilots Association (PALPA), Society of Aircraft Engineers of Pakistan (SAEP), PIA's Senior Staff Association (PIASSA), Peoples Unity, Collective Bargaining Agent (CBA), and Aircraft Technologist Association of Pakistan (ATAP) are some examples. Different political parties back different unions. This union system is a major impediment in laying off unnecessary workers or implementing other efficiency measures. For example, when the PML-N government announced the selling of 26 per cent of PIA's share to kickstart the privatization process, CBA threatened to launch countrywide protests.

The unions have become so powerful that in recent cases, they have even forced the resignation of people in top positions, including the managing director. Aijaz Haroon, a serving pilot who was appointed MD by the PPP government in 2008, was forced to resign in 2011 by the protests of PALPA, which did not agree with Haroon's decision of sharing routes with Turkish Airlines. Another unhealthy development that has surfaced is the appointment of pilots to top management positions due to the excessive influence of PALPA. Since 2008, serving pilots have been repeatedly getting the top position of managing director.[2] Management, especially of an airline company is a highly specialized field for experienced aviation-management experts, rather than pilots who are specialists in a completely different field, that is flying airplanes. Two successful examples of strong leadership are Idris Jala, the former CEO of Malaysian Airlines, and Kazuo Inamora, who revived Japan Airlines; both were from the private sector without any experience in aviation.

Leadership issues also crop up in terms of the short tenure of the top management of PIA, which is changed on the basis of political considerations. This does not allow the top management to focus on the long-term structural issues of the airline.

• **Poor regulatory arrangements**: Certain problems leading to the current state of PIA are linked to the absence of a proper regulatory framework. It is the responsibility of the regulator to ensure that an aircraft is fit for flying, and that it conforms to international laws. The Civil Aviation Authority (CAA) is the regulatory body for all airlines in Pakistan, including PIA. CAA's official statement indicates that:

The purpose of establishing CAA is to provide for the promotion and regulations of Civil Aviation activities and to develop an infrastructure for safe, efficient, adequate, economical, and properly coordinated civil air transport service in Pakistan.[3]

The frequency of technical faults, crash landings, and air accidents of PIA indicate the failure of CAA in investigating these accidents and reporting their findings. Over the period 1956–2014, PIA planes have suffered a total of 47 accidents, implying an average of around 0.8 accidents per year.[4] In 2006, the European Union banned PIA's Airbus fleet from entering EU routes because of failure to meet its safety standards. While the ban was lifted a year later, PIA suffered a loss of PKR13 billion that year.

Why is CAA unable to adequately regulate PIA? The answer lies in the absence of the independence of CAA. By definition, a regulatory body needs to be completely insulated from any type of influence from the entity that it is expected to regulate. However, this is not true of the relationship between CAA and PIA. As an example, in September 2010, Nadeem Khan Yousafzai, a serving pilot of PIA at that time, was appointed as director general of CAA. He stayed in that position until February 2011, when he was appointed managing director of PIA. Almost a year later, he was reappointed as director general of CAA. In other words, CAA has been led by an employee of one of the clients.

These shifts from top position in CAA to PIA and back to CAA, with periods when he was holding both positions is a classic case of conflict of interest. There are other such examples both at the top management and lower levels.

Since coming to power in 2013, the PML-N government placed PIA, CAA and Airport Security Force (ASF) under a newly created Aviation Division reporting to the aviation advisor and to the prime minister. Previously, these three entities were under the control of the Defence Ministry.[5] However, this has not made CAA any more independent, with the head of the Aviation Division practically heading CAA and PIA. To make PIA more efficient, the first step on the regulatory front would be to make CAA an independent and autonomous body in both letter and spirit. The employees, and specifically the head of CAA, should be completely buffered from its clients—the airlines—whose regulation is the key task of CAA.

In short, the critical situation of PIA is the result of excessive political interference, particularly in hiring and firing decisions, which have led to massive overstaffing. It is also the result of leadership issues and excessively aggressive trade unions. And finally it is the result of the poor regulatory regime undertaken by CAA.

PAKISTAN RAILWAY (PR)—A STATE OF SECULAR DECLINE

The Railway in pre-Partition British India was a symbol of modernity, enterprise, and power of colonial rule. The first major shock to the nascent PR came at the time of partition in 1947 when most of the trained officers and engineers of the Indian Railway migrated to India. However, the organization was able to withstand this shock and to grow during the first two decades, achieving satisfactory levels of passenger and freight service. This growth soon petered out, and PR failed to galvanize on the economic opportunities of subsequent decades. Since the 1990s, PR has seen a secular decline in almost all parameters of performance and efficiency. Today the organization is a symbol of all that is diametrically opposed to modernity, enterprise and power. It has acquired a reputation for being persistently unpunctual, painfully slow, and woefully obsolete in its technology.[6]

The financial predicaments of PR have less to do with the general state of Pakistan's economy, rather it is chronic mismanagement that has plagued PR. While GDP growth averaged 4–5 per cent a year, over the past three decades, and population grew around 2 per cent a year, this rise in income and population should have translated into an increase in demand for railway services. In fact, with some 80 per cent of Pakistan's population and economic activity being within 50 km of the main railway line, the normal expectations would have been for PR to grow rather than shrink and deteriorate in terms of operational scale and service.[7]

Pakistan Railway is perhaps the only railway system in the world which has seen a reduction in track length over time. Of the roughly 5,050 miles of railway line that was inherited in good condition in 1947, only about

4,840 remains.[8] Similarly, passenger service in 2013 had fallen from 230 to 92 trains per day, and the number of freight trains went down from 96 to merely one train a day.[9] A major reason behind the rapid deterioration of railway service has been the lack of availability of locomotives/engines. Since 2011, the number of functional locomotives available for use has persistently decreased at an average of 10 per month.[10] In 2013, PR had about 420 locomotives on paper, but there were only a 100 which were operational. The decline in the number of functional locomotives has severely compromised the efficiency and effectiveness of the network of train service across the entire country. Complicating the matter further, of the 100 operational locomotives, the relatively new Chinese engines are considered less reliable in comparison to the older US engines, increasing the cost of maintenance and the probability of breakdowns—the single most important factor behind the frequent and inordinate train delays.

In an attempt to lessen the impact of the decline in functional locomotives on train passenger service, locomotives were diverted from freight to passenger service. This led to a dramatic fall in freight service—a major source of revenue for PR because of its relatively lower overheads and operational costs.[11] Not surprisingly, PR's share of inland freight traffic fell from 73 per cent to only 4 per cent.[12] What was once the largest transport network of the country has shrunk in significance and market share to a burgeoning road transportation sector.

Underlying the decline in PR's operations and performance is a state of pervasive financial crisis. The annual earnings of PR have consistently declined between the fiscal periods 2009–10 and 2014–15. The only exception has been the fiscal year 2012–13, during which earnings increased by 17 per cent.[13] Despite this increase, PR still ran a PKR31 billion deficit that year, due to high operational costs.[14] Often the government had to step in to rescue the organization from its state of perpetual insolvency. Like other state-owned enterprises, PR was supposed to have been privatized during the 1990s as part of a broader structural adjustment framework. However, since then the prescription has changed to a public-private partnership to lessen its burden on the national exchequer.

Several factors have contributed to the decline of PR. These include: a bias against investment in PR in favour of road transport; excessive labour force, corruption, and inappropriate resource management; organizational structure and political interference; and financial mismanagement and lack of planning.

- **Roads versus railways; A policy decision:** PR has historically suffered from neglect and a sustained lack of public investment. This is a direct consequence of policies which have consistently favoured roads and related transport network over railways. For example, in the last three years, the allocation to PR has been approximately half the amount allocated to the National Highway Authority.[15] This has been the trend since the First Five-Year Plan, which saw the construction of 1,800 miles of new roads and the renovation of 2,000 miles of existing roads. Although the disproportionate investment in roads and related transport networks seems to have been a clear policy choice, there has also been a rent seeking incentive on the part of successive governments behind the construction of roads at the expense of investments in railways. In the past there have been serious allegations of conflict of interest at the highest level in the Railway Ministry which might have contributed to the systemic mismanagement and deliberate neglect of the railway service. The provision of subsidized diesel to trucks and buses under Ayub Khan's regime, and the establishment of the National Logistics Cell (NLC) under Zia ul-Haq's government only exacerbated the problems of PR. NLC is the largest food transportation company in the country, and has the largest public sector transport fleet in Asia.[16] Heads of the four main divisions of the NLC and the ground operations staff are all drawn from the military, leaving civilians to perform only administrative and clerical roles. Dr Ayesha Siddiqa has argued that under the pretext of creating a more efficient organization, the military created a 'duplication of efforts,' and strengthened the NLC instead of reviving Pakistan Railway, by extending to the NLC the patronage that is part and parcel of being associated with the military in Pakistan.[17] In short, the decline in railways reflects a vicious cycle: A pro-road transport policy that diverted resources away from the railways, and the resulting

deteriorating passenger and freight service that led to
reduced revenues and demand.

• **Overstaffing, corruption, and inappropriate resource
  management**: Pakistan Railway is the largest public
  sector employer in Pakistan, with more than 80,000
  employees. Given the financial fragility of the
  organization, workers are often in a state of protest
  as a consequence of delayed or unpaid salaries. This
  overstaffing has serious ramifications; for example in
  2013–14, PR's gross earnings (PKR22.8 billion) were
  just enough to cover wages and salaries. There have
  been some efforts in the past to downsize PR and
  make it financially sustainable. In 2002, a voluntary
  separation scheme resulted in a decline of 50,000 in
  employees. However, after ten years of the downsizing
  campaign, PR was again on the verge of bankruptcy.
  A fundamental reason for this is the disproportionate
  increase in the number of workers in departments
  and areas of the organization (stores, police, and
  headquarters) which have minimal impact on
  improving PR's service.[18] Moreover, PR has also had
  to incur huge financial costs on account of pensions
  of former employees. For example, in 2013–14, the
  pension cost of PR was about PKR15 billion, more
  than half of the payroll cost of employees.[19]

Owing partly to under or unpaid employees, and
partly to an inadequate oversight of the institution,
PR is a victim to endemic corruption. Employees and
officials have been reported to steal rails, sleepers,

and other supplies. Several bridges have collapsed, thus halting operations, while new bridges are constructed using poor material—and it is only a matter of time before they too collapse.[20] Given the overemployment at a time of trains being seldom used, most of the employees stay at home and receive wages illegitimately. Others performing clerical work would review and process no more than one file in an eight-hour shift.[21] Recruitment of these employees is ascertained by political patronage, bribery, and nepotism rather than organizational needs and personal skills. Meanwhile the powerful unions of the railway industry vociferously fight any attempt to reduce overstaffing or employee benefits.[22]

Corruption is not restricted to the lower layers of the hierarchy but is also pervasive among the higher echelons of power. For instance, in the recent past coaches and engines were imported from China, despite the fact that Pakistan manufactures coaches locally, and houses a locomotive assembly plant. These purchased locomotives did not meet the specifications of PR.[23] This did not succeed in deterring the purchase, and reportedly many of the purchased locomotives are currently non-functional.

There is also a pattern of corruption in the management of PR's land assets. Railway land was sold to a group of businessmen at low prices and was used to construct the Royal Palm Golf and Country Club—a 'lavish facility with an 18-hole golf course, gyms, 3D cinemas, cigar rooms', and a USD8,000 membership fee.[24] The National AccountabilityBureau (NAB) concluded that the Royal Palm deal cost PR millions of dollars in lost revenue.

Further aggravating the situation, the railway accounts are not subject to checks by the Auditor General of Pakistan, and PR is not a member of the International Union of Railways—the international standards regulatory authority. These factors reduce accountability and increase the opportunities for corruption and mismanagement. Businesses and passengers prefer relying on more competitive private transporters or efficient alternatives such as NLC, instead of dealing with an inefficient and corrupt bureaucracy such as PR.

- **Lack of autonomy and political interference**: Many of PR's problems stem from the fact that it is subjected to significant interference from the federal government and lacks a fully autonomous institutional structure. From 1960s onwards, PR was run by an autonomous four-member board. The board was composed of a member traffic, member mechanical, member civil, and member finance. While the Ministry of Finance made one of the nominations to the board, senior railway officers that were experts in their respective fields filled the remaining three positions. Even though the federal government appointed the chairman, the choice had to be from one of the three technical fields. This allowed PR to operate as a relatively autonomous, self-sustaining organization. However, in 1982 the Railway Board was merged with the Ministry of Railways and the 'locus of power and authority shifted to the Federal Secretariat in Islamabad'.[25] Later in 1990, the government appointed a member of the Pakistan civil service, with no prior railway experience, as chairman of PR—and with that began an era of persistent federal government interference in the affairs of PR. Thereafter, decisions began to be made much more on the basis of political considerations rather than economic efficiency. Trains were run to and from the minister's constituency at the expense of other routes. Economic and financial feasibility studies were conveniently waived. Railway stations were built to serve the political interests of parliamentarians, and once built, political pressure was applied to maximize the number of trains stopping at those stations. All this meant a tremendous increase in both overhead and operations costs of PR without any significant revenue generation.

- **Financial mismanagement and lack of planning**: The financial management of PR is bifurcated into two independent departments—revenue and expense. The general manager for revenue and the general manager for expenditure work in their 'silos', with minimal interdepartmental coordination or interaction. The main objective of the revenue department is the collection and reconciliation of revenue from ticket sales across all train stations in the country. Except for forty railway stations where ticket issuance and seat reservation for a particular train is computerized, the rest of the stations have no data linking passenger revenues to either trains or to train routes.[26] The revenue department therefore has no information on the financial viability of a particular train service or train route. Nor does the department feel the need to compare train ticket pricing to that of its competitors. According to interviews conducted for a LUMS case study on PR, the revenue department does not consider this as being part of its domain of activities, and instead ascribed the responsibility for such information gathering and analysis to the Traffic and Commercial department. The latter in turn had estimates of passenger revenue on some train routes, which on further inquiry were more conjectural than based on any rigorous data collection exercise. What is clearly evident from the LUMS case study is that the limited ambit of operations of each of these departments, lack of interdepartmental coordination, and severe limitations of capacity do not allow any financial planning or analysis of the feasibility of train services or train routes.

Furthermore, there is no department in the overall organizational structure that is dedicated to research and development. This has a major impact on the way decisions are taken on running new trains. While running a new train costs somewhere between PKR200 million to PKR500 million, no market research is undertaken to test the feasibility of such a costly investment.[27] Effectively, the decision on such a large investment hinges on a trial-and-error process characteristic of PR in general.

To conclude, Pakistan Railway is in a dire state of financial and organizational crisis. Successive governments' neglect of the development of railways, the prevalence of corruption and rent-seeking at all levels of PR, a culture of political interference and patronage that has led to unabated hiring in already overstaffed and inefficient departments, and the absence of institutional autonomy and interdepartmental coordination have aggravated the problems of PR.

The problems of PR are not insurmountable, but they will need to be addressed boldly and in a comprehensive manner. Significantly large investments in both track and rolling stock will be required to relieve the existing supply constraints stifling both passenger and freight services. This should be viewed in the context of greater regional connectivity that would be made possible by the proposed Pakistan China Economic Corridor. A reinvigorated PR would multiply the efficiency gains and economic rents of the corridor by significantly reducing transport costs of an expected high volume of freight traffic.

After sixty-eight years, PR also needs to graduate from being an importer of engines and coaches to becoming a manufacturer. Joint ventures with companies such as General Electric (GE), eventually leading to skills and technology transfer, would be a step in the right direction. Such investments would not only make the organization technologically adept and self-sufficient, but would also lead to beneficial externalities in other sectors of the economy.

It will also be important for the incentive structure in PR to undergo reform so that the problems of corruption are addressed. A revision of employee salaries, supported by adjustments in the workforce to reduce unproductive workers, would help. This should be accompanied by a fundamental change in the structure of the organization to make it immune to political pressures.

Finally, to sustain efficient decision-making, it is important to provide a degree of organizational and financial autonomy to PR so that its management, administration and decision-making are less politicized. Whatever structure replaces the existing one, it is imperative that Pakistan Railway be granted greater institutional autonomy to end the politicization and rent-seeking within the institution. A more decentralized and autonomous system where professional managers are not burdened with political pressures nor preoccupied with the need to concentrate power in their own hands, will better serve the interests of Pakistan Railway and the country.

13

The Underpinnings of Success

The preceding chapters have provided details on the factors of success and the remaining challenges of the nine organizations in our sample, as well as the factors behind the failures of two public organizations. Many of the factors are common to these institutions, but there are also some specific factors.

In this chapter, we bring together the main factors that assured the success of these organizations. Many of these factors were highlighted in the general discussion in chapter two.

CLEAR OBJECTIVES AND GOALS

Experience with the performance of organizations indicates that those with clear and specific vision statements and focus are more likely to achieve their objectives. Entities that are burdened with multiple and conflicting goals are hampered in attaining their goals.

The outputs and outcomes of **LUMS** are routinely measured and assessed. Some of the indicators measured are research produced and published in reputable journals, teaching evaluation and teaching material developed, case studies developed, research funding generated, consultancy work undertaken, conferences attended, and training undertaken. Teaching evaluation of the faculty is publicly available on the university website. These clear and measurable goals are documented and reviewed by the Faculty Appointment and Promotion Committee (FAPC) or school tenure committees, and in annual faculty appraisals.

In the case of **Shaukat Khanum Cancer Hospital**, to ensure quality provision of services, each department has its own set of efficiency goals and measures or benchmarks for its staff at both the individual and departmental levels. Some examples of these benchmarks are the percentage of people getting free treatment, delivery of quality care, percentage of on-time reports in the pathology and radiology departments, cost and the returns of fundraising, turnover in human resources, etc. An effort is made to make these departmental benchmarks comparable to prevailing international standards in the health industry. Where a relevant international standard is not available, the department is encouraged to come up with its own measure, which is tracked over time. The performance of the departments is shared regularly in hospital operations meetings. Similarly, on the clinical side, there is an executive board that monitors internationally recognized clinical benchmarks such as infection rates, average length of stay, readmission after surgery, etc. There are also external goals. For example, the hospital has applied for a premium external accreditation known as the Joint Commission International. The current security situation in the country prohibits the commission from visiting the hospital. However, hospital management is confident that it would receive accreditation without any problem. Apart from this, there are several agencies, such as the Pakistan Centre for Philanthropy and A. F. Ferguson that undertake the hospital's audit on a periodic basis. Pakistan Nuclear Regulatory Authority (PNRA) keeps a check on radiation safety measures and there is an audit of food services as well.

NADRA's mission, as laid out in the 2000 ordinance establishing it and also in the revised vision statement of 2006, is very clear, specific, and achievable. It is not burdened with peripheral objectives that would detract it from its core objectives.

The objective of **Rescue 1122** is very clear and unequivocal: To provide high quality emergency service to citizens of Pakistan. To ensure timely delivery of quality service, a response time of less than seven minutes was chosen as a performance standard.

ATTRACTING AND RETAINING SKILLED STAFF

There is no doubt that the success of an organization depends on the competence and dedication of its staff. A common characteristic of the analysed organizations is that they have been able to mobilize and build on existing skills, competitively recruit senior and middle management staff and train new employees, and retain them in the medium- and long-term. Access to training and international exposure has been important in attracting and retaining competitive candidates.

The faculty at **LUMS** is young and energetic, with over 80 per cent holding doctoral degrees. In the business school portion of the institution, professors received training in the case method early on from foreign professors. Overall, there has been strong peer pressure on the faculty to undertake research, aided by a generally low teaching load in comparison to other private sector colleges and universities in the country. More research time is also complemented by generous research funds/grants. The faculty is also involved in providing consulting advice to the federal and local governments as well as to international donors.

There has been some turnover of faculty, but generally LUMS has been able to retain and attract new faculty across various disciplines. LUMS administrative staff is provided regular in-house training to improve their work performance and skill set.

Similar to LUMS, a great deal of stress is placed on the quality of staff at **IBA**. Clear guidelines and benchmarks are established for faculty selection. Qualifications are reviewed; presentation to the faculty is required; and an interview with the dean is arranged. Student evaluation of teachers is considered important, and consistently poor evaluations can be problematic for the faculty member. Staff members are required to go abroad for exposure to international experience. IBA also ensures that faculty who return from trainings, workshops, or conferences abroad share and disseminate the knowledge they gained with the rest of the faculty. All this is in addition to relatively good remuneration for the staff.

In the case of the **Motorway Police**, selection and recruitment are purely merit-based. Application requirements are explicit, and tests are held simultaneously at all centres. There is video coverage of physical fitness and written examinations. The interview committee is headed by the inspector general of police, and assignments to new posts are merit-based.

There are numerous incentives to attract and retain quality police officers. Pay scales are about 30–40 per cent higher than in other police forces in the country. There are also welfare benefits, including free bachelor accommodation, proper mess arrangements, health allowance and indoor/outdoor sports facilities, scholarships, financial assistance for daughters' marriages, burial assistance, welfare petrol pumps, and special employment quotas for children of officers killed in service.

At **Rescue 1122**, clear and transparent guidelines are in place for hiring and firing staff, and there have been instances of lay-offs when performance levels dipped below par. The practice of hiring staff on a permanent rather than contractual basis is a relatively recent development. Although the greater job security initially led to some laxity in staff performance, this was quickly rectified with the introduction of more rigorous performance measures. The organization's management by objectives strategy, whereby employees set their own goals, has allowed for a high degree of objectivity in employee performance appraisal, uncommon to most public sector institutions. Moreover, this strategy has enhanced employee performance by circumventing the apprehension and dissatisfaction that stem from unclear job expectations. Clarity in job descriptions and the fact that employees know precisely what is expected of them results in better planning and target setting, better communications between managers and staff, and consequently better retention of staff.

From the start, Dr Rizwan Naseer implemented carefully designed policies and procedures for hiring that would ensure selection on merit. The post-selection six-month training course at the Rescue 1122 Academy was designed to be a rigorous programme, which would sift out those not suitable for the organization. The implementation of this two-tiered selection process—examination/selection and training—was an effective protection mechanism against any form of political interference in employment decisions.

Being a part of the public sector, the prevailing employee pay scales at Rescue 1122 are no different from any other public sector organization. However, there are monetary bonuses and rewards which are given to employees based on their performance. The initial selection procedure ensures that the staff hired meets a minimum criterion, while periodic on-the-job training helps improve the capacity and efficiency of the staff. Interestingly, Rescue 1122 has a relatively low employee turnover rate, which signals both worker efficiency and job satisfaction. In fact, the original management team is still intact, including, of course, Dr Naseer.

The continuity of association and service of senior management has been a major factor in the success of the organization from its pilot phase. With decentralization of operational management, the planning and strategy side of Rescue 1122 is also shared and democratic. Periodic meetings, training, and motivational sessions allow managers and employees to have a say in the future growth and strategic vision of the organization. This culture of openness and ownership at all levels is critical in ensuring the continued success of Rescue 1122.

In the case of **NADRA**, it has been blessed with an effective workforce, which is young (average age between 30–40 years for most functions), dynamic, non-bureaucratic, entrepreneurial, and which sees change as a perpetual fact of life at the workplace. Staff work under overall long-term objectives but are also devising short-term solutions and firefighting on a day-to-day basis. NADRA also has the most computer literate workforce in the country. All this is helped by the fact that it has competitive compensation and benefits, especially for technical employees, who are compensated at prevailing market rates, which are much higher than those for operational workers.

A key challenge for **Shaukat Khanum Cancer Hospital's** administration has been to hire qualified staff who meet the requisite standards (the hospital has a total strength of 1,800 employees, consisting of consultant staff, residents, nursing staff, and related medical support staff). While efficient service delivery has become the hallmark of the institution, this has been a consequence of a highly selective recruitment strategy. The country's limited investment in training healthcare workers has generated a serious shortfall of nurses, paramedics, laboratory and surgical assistants, as well as management and public health experts. This has complicated matters for institutions such as Shaukat Khanum, which aims to employ well-trained professionals across all levels of operation.

The hiring processes of the human resource team of Shaukat Khanum are transparent and purely merit-based, with no room for any type of influence or interference. The management maintains that the prevailing salary structure is competitive, with annual performance-based appraisals. In order to provide incentives to doctors and specialists, the remunerations and annual pay increases are based on the quantity and quality of work done, i.e. research, clinical output, teaching, etc. Moreover, the hospital provides complete health coverage/insurance to all its employees—a major factor behind the claimed high retention.

The hospital employs highly qualified UK and US-trained physicians who draw on a multidisciplinary approach to administer world-class diagnostic treatment and support services to cancer patients. The institution has capitalized heavily on the cumulative know-how of experienced staff members, and the notably high employee retention rate has ensured that gains from extensive staff training are preserved.

FINANCIAL SUSTAINABILITY

Central to the success of any institution is adequate and stable funding. Without this, the organization will be heavily dependent on government resources and, hence subject to public interference in the day-to-day business of the entity.

In the case of **LUMS**, the core funding was provided by the initial five to six National Management Foundation donors. The pro-vice chancellor, Syed Babar Ali, was active in seeking foreign funding for the university from USAID and The Rausing Trust. Initially, some 70 per cent of the expenses were funded from outside sources. Now own funding is the predominant source. Tuition fees alone cover between 60–70 per cent of the costs. This is a relatively high ratio in comparison to some international universities.[1]

For **IBA**, financial sustainability seems well assured, with the share of tuition fees in total receipts increasing from around 40 per cent in 2007–08 to 51 per cent in 2011–12. Reliance on government grants, while important (about 16 per cent of total), is not the main source of income. Also, increased enrolment (enabled by enhanced infrastructure) will help improve financial sustainability. This satisfactory financial position makes the institution more immune to government interventions, assisted by its independent board of directors.

Punjab Education Fund (PEF) is a very good example of lean and efficient public sector management where most of the resources are directly spent on programmes rather than on administration. Of the allocated budget, about 95 per cent goes into programmes, with only 2 per cent going into programme-related expenditures and only 3 per cent being used for administrative or general purposes. PEF management ensures that the administrative costs are kept at a minimum so that maximum resources might be directed toward the foundation's programmes.

PEF also depends heavily on international donors such as the World Bank, Canadian International Development Agency (CIDA), and DFID. This dependence on foreign funds raises issues of future financial sustainability, especially after the tapering off of World Bank funds after 2017. However, recently the Punjab government has shown its commitment towards PEF by allocating resources towards its programmes in the annual budget. This ownership of the government is a positive sign in terms of ensuring financial sustainability of the organization.

In contrast to other organizations in our sample, **Edhi Foundation** has had a consistent policy of not taking donations or resources of any kind from either the government or international agencies. This policy has resulted in the organization's being insulated from and independent of external pressures and interference. At the same time, this independence has helped build the necessary legitimacy, trust, and credibility within the general public, which remains the organization's main source of funds and donations. Shunning governmental and international donors' funds has also enabled it to maintain autonomy and to avoid red tape.[2]

Rescue 1122 is a provincial entity and hence subject to the budgetary provision of the government. The organization is moving towards empowering local communities to respond to their own medical emergencies through extensive training programmes. This effort is aimed at reducing the scope of manpower resources of the organization and laying the groundwork for community responses to local emergencies. The organization has also focused on indigenous manufacture and repair as part of its cost-cutting strategy. These endeavours have been helpful to the organization in reducing financial distress. Interestingly, one reason cited for the organization's insularity from local-level extortion and patronage networks is not just its credibility and reputation but also a recognized paucity of any extra funds to pay off local touts and mafias.

In the case of **Shaukat Khanum Memorial Cancer Hospital**, almost 50 per cent of the revenue generated comes from overseas and domestic donations including zakat funds. The rest is raised from medical services provided by the hospital. To tap into the donor base, the marketing department of the hospital has come up with innovative methods of fundraising which include regular fundraising events/dinners, SMS and online donation services, periodic countrywide fundraising drives, school and college campaigns, etc. The finance department of the hospital is gradually moving away from a donor-driven model to a more sustainable strategy of investment in a diverse range of assets and financial instruments, locally and internationally.

Vision and Continuity of Leadership

As with most organizations in the world, a key requisite for success is strong leadership that has a clear vision of the organization's mission and goals, and a clearly articulated process to translate the vision into concrete programmes and targets. It requires a leadership that has the ability to raise funding for the institution and empowers management and staff to perform their functions within the established framework, while also buffering the organization against unnecessary outside interventions.

A critically important factor in the success of **LUMS**, especially in its formative years, was the quality of its leadership. The pro-vice chancellor of LUMS, Syed Babar Ali, is a successful, highly respected, and internationally known corporate leader of the country. He perceived the need and the opportunity for an institution that would meet the industry's demand for good managers and leaders. His international stature was critically important, both for funding to attract and retain competent staff, and for exposure of the faculty and students to the business community. Business leaders were invited to lecture, and field visits were arranged for students. Quality staff was selected so that even with just about a dozen faculty members in its earlier days, the institution became recognized for quality and went beyond the original proposal of being a training centre. All this would have been impossible without the leadership of Syed Babar Ali.

Syed Babar Ali has also been a great delegator. While he kept himself well-informed and focused on the big picture matters, he left a great deal to the first director of LUMS, Javed Hamid, who had moved temporarily to LUMS from the International Finance Corporation (IFC) of the World Bank Group. Mr Hamid's experience at the Harvard Business School led him to recommend the use of the case method of teaching, and Syed Babar Ali bought into the proposal. It is interesting that the design of the new campus and the method of teaching were dictated at least in part by the adoption of the case method.

Finally, Syed Babar Ali was also instrumental in acquiring foreign funding for the university from The Rausing Trust and USAID. In its earlier years, almost 70 per cent of the expenses were funded from outside sources.

A critically important factor for the success of **IBA** as an institution has been the sustained leadership during its formative 'golden' years during the 1950s and early 1960s, as well as its more recent visionary and proactive leadership. As the first business school in Pakistan, it was blessed with competent management, which stayed for sufficient time in office to provide the continuity needed in the early years. For example, during the almost thirty-year period from 1954 to 1984, only three deans/directors held office. IBA fell on difficult times in the late 1990s and early 2000s, but since 2002—and more specifically since 2008—the institution has had remarkably successful leadership. Mr Danishmand—the dean/director from 2002–2008— steadied the decline during his tenure and helped rebuild the reputation of IBA. However, the real turnaround took place after Dr Ishrat Husain was appointed the dean/

director in 2008. Highly-respected in the country for his successful stint as governor of the State Bank of Pakistan, and internationally recognized as a scholar and strong manager, he addressed the key issues confronting IBA.

Dr Husain provided the leadership IBA desperately needed at a critical time for the institution. He developed, in a participatory manner, a longer-term vision for IBA. He instituted regular weekly meetings in a collegial atmosphere of the executive committee, where decisions were taken as a unified team. He developed the IBA code book, which incorporates in a single document all the relevant rules and regulations at IBA and which is regularly updated. He improved the working conditions and salaries of staff. Also, given his reputation with the private sector in Karachi, he was able to raise large donations for upgrading the badly depreciated building and information technology infrastructure. In short, he brought a change of culture and excitement to the institution.

The leadership provided at a crucial time had a significant positive impact on IBA. In line with the institute's vision of becoming one of the top ten business schools in South Asia, it received in 2011 the accreditation of the South Asia Quality Assurance System (SAQS). IBA is now one of only two business schools in Pakistan (the other is LUMS) to have achieved this distinction.

The **Motorway Police** has similarly been fortunate to have effective top leadership, with inspectors general such as Zia ul Hasan and Wasim Kausar, who played key roles in the development of the police force. Given this leadership, the organization had little interference from any quarter in the performance of its duties.

The top leadership in **NADRA** has been equally strong and involved. The leader of the organization cuts across hierarchical boundaries and obtains feedback directly from the middle management in a participative manner. What makes NADRA unique is its ability to balance a democratic culture with an autocratic culture. Once decisions are made on the broad objectives and standards, the technical staff is given ample leeway to perform their functions. On the other hand, NADRA also has retired senior military officials in its management who follow a more hierarchical structure and approach. As a result, for some departments, power distances are high, the approach is more collectivist, and risk-taking is lower. By contrast, other departments exhibit participative styles of management and are marked by flatter organization. The point is that these two management styles coexist side by side under the overall leadership of the chairman.

The leadership of **Edhi Foundation** is unique. Set up in 1951, perhaps the most enduring reason for its success is the degree of credibility and legitimacy it has enjoyed since its inception. Although generally institutional success rests on the extent and ability of its being independent of an individual figure or founder, Edhi presents a unique and somewhat anomalous case of an exception to this well-established rule. Abdul Sattar Edhi's unassuming and humble personality and his incorruptible character and simple lifestyle betray the importance the man garners as the founder and chief executive of the largest philanthropic organization in the country. The almost saintly persona of Edhi has helped galvanize a large and continually increasing donor base.

Along with the powerful image of simplicity, the remarkable dedication and zeal of Abdul Sattar Edhi in helping the poor and the marginalized over the past decades has been a key factor behind establishing social trust and ownership. This is a case where it is difficult to separate the organization from the person of Edhi, both in terms of the organizational image he helped create and the central role he continues to play in running the foundation. It is also difficult to predict whether the public trust in the foundation has permeated beyond the individual to the organization itself. Given the deeply symbiotic relationship between Edhi and his organization, a serious future challenge would be to maintain the same degree of support and donation from the public after his lifetime. The foundation operates on a central management structure that entails few lines of authority between management and staff. There is no middle-level management in the organization and high-level 'circle managers' run the day-to-day administration, and collaborate directly with employees and customers. With his son, Faisal Edhi, as the vice chairman and other family members as directors, the philanthropist approves all projects personally and retains final say in all decisions, from the most significant to the least. This highly centralized management strategy is based on Edhi's belief that having one person in the driver's seat prevents degeneration in mission drift, and ensures consistency in decision-making. In short, Edhi's failing health raises the issue of sustainability of the organization after his death.

For **Rescue 1122**, the dedication and dogged determination of Dr Rizwan Naseer, the first director general, and his team was instrumental in the establishment of the organization. Dr Naseer, an orthopedic surgeon, was able to successfully launch his entrepreneurial initiative after almost a decade attempting to reform the Civil Defense Authority (CDA) of the federal government. Rescue 1122 evolved quickly from a small-scale Lahore Pilot Project into an institution with operations spread across the Punjab province. This was a hard won victory for a team of dedicated professionals determined to fill the void in quality emergency service provision. As a result of this timely leadership, to date, Rescue 1122's fleet of ambulances have handled over 400,000 victims across Punjab, and the services rendered include disaster response, road traffic accident management, fire and water rescue services, and community safety programmes.

Since the pilot phase to the rapid expansion across the province, Dr Naseer has led the organization by being at the forefront of all its activities. From management and planning, to being physically part of rescue operations, to taking the lead in staff training and exercises, he is a hands-on director general who has led by example. The exemplary leadership has been a critical factor in ensuring the success of Rescue 1122. It has helped establish a culture of service delivery within the organization and at the same time is a huge motivational factor for the management and staff.

Among specialized private sector hospitals in the country, the **Shaukat Khanum Memorial Cancer Hospital** is arguably one of the most well-functioning, integrated tertiary healthcare facilities in Pakistan. In fact, in comparison to the other private and public organizations reviewed in this study, Shaukat Khanum stands out as exemplary in terms of both overall success in meeting its vision and maintaining a high standard of service delivery. The individual behind the idea of establishing a state-of-the-art cancer hospital that would provide free treatment to the poor was Imran Khan, the founder of the hospital and famous cricketer-turned-politician.

Establishing a research hospital in a developing country which would dispense world-class cancer treatment on a need-blind basis, train healthcare professionals in the latest medical developments, and conduct state-of-the-art cancer research was a highly ambitious endeavour and many experts were understandably sceptical of its feasibility. Against all reasoned opinions and odds, Imran Khan and a small but dedicated team of friends and doctors persevered and led one of the most successful fundraising campaigns in the country's history. It took three years to raise the requisite amount of USD22 million for the first phase of the hospital. Two important factors lay behind this remarkably successful fundraising campaign. The first and most obvious was Imran Khan's celebrity status within and outside Pakistan. The victory of Pakistan's cricket team in the World Cup of 1992, led by none other than Imran Khan, played a major role in galvanizing unprecedented support for the hospital. The second was the organization and management of the fundraising campaign, which was able to target different segments of society very effectively—people from different income and demographic groups within the country, as well as from an increasingly wealthy Pakistani diaspora.

MANAGERIAL AUTONOMY AND POLITICAL SUPPORT

An important factor in the success of **LUMS** is the arms-length arrangement that has been maintained between the Management Committee and university administration.[3] Unlike some other academic institutions in Pakistan and elsewhere, it is not a family-run institution. Within the framework established, faculty and staff are empowered to take decisions on day-to-day matters. Also, as the university has grown—with four different schools—the structure of administration and management has devolved considerably to the various schools. More recently, LUMS has moved towards a model of shared governance. This entails an elected faculty council responsible for academic policies, standards, and issues. The Management Committee plays a role only in terms of setting the broader agenda and vision for future growth.

Similarly, despite being a public institution, **IBA** has remained immune to government intervention. It has an independent board of directors with members drawn from both the public and private sectors.

In the case of **BISP**, the strong and widespread political support for it has been an important factor in its establishment and continuation of the programme. This support has continued even with changes of government. The document that formed the basis of BISP—the National Social Protection Strategy of 2007—was prepared under the Musharraf regime. During the Pakistan Peoples Party's (PPP) government that followed, strong support was ensured to the organization, with the then president of the country meeting with the chairperson of BISP twice a month. Even the change in government in 2013 from PPP to PML-N did not diminish support for the programme. In fact, the new government has continued to increase the budgetary support to BISP, even though two chairpersons were replaced over a period of about two years.

Apart from government and all political parties' commitment to the programme, substantial autonomy was delegated to BISP. The programme has its own chairman and its own board of directors, 50 per cent of whom are from the private sector. The board has also played a positive role, especially in the areas of finance, auditing, and human resource management.

A set of carefully delineated guidelines and procedural details served to insulate **Rescue 1122** from political patronage over employment decisions and to guard undue, politically motivated interference in its general day-to-day operations. Rescue 1122 had double cause to be careful in formulating rules and protocols because of its high cost and public funding. It needed to placate the ruling political party and public officials, so as to survive politically as well as financially. The procedures put in place in the human resource department of the organization are a good example of institutional rules that insulated Rescue 1122 from pressures of political patronage and nepotism. The rigorous recruitment requirements succeeded in sifting out all but the fittest for the job, and the gruelling six-month training period further filtered any ill-suited workers. The director general was able to convince those at the helm of provincial affairs that a well-performing and professionally-run public sector enterprise, known for its service, integrity, and work ethic, was a more viable political asset than a political organization smeared with allegations of corruption and inefficiency. The provincial government demonstrated its confidence in the organization by readily allocating the needed funds to it.

The management structure of **Shaukat Khanum** is decentralized. There is a board of governors on top of the organizational hierarchy followed by a CEO and various departmental heads. The role of each tier of the organizational pyramid is carefully delineated. The board does not interfere in the day-to-day management and operations of the hospital, which is left to the CEO and the departmental heads.

What is noteworthy, and also different from other organizations, is the role played by the founder, Imran

Khan. Although he is a permanent member of the board of governors, he does not interfere in the management and organization of the hospital except for assistance in fundraising campaigns. This is why Shaukat Khanum Hospital's identity is independent of the person of Imran Khan—which is precisely what makes the hospital an 'institution'.

The **Punjab Education Foundation** is a well-functioning autonomous government organization under the provincial education ministry, established to encourage and promote education through various programmes of public and private partnership. The management of the foundation is decentralized and vertical. There is a board of directors under which function the various committees and administrative departments. A key success factor for the institution is the fact that it is autonomous of the provincial education ministry in terms of having an independent and competent board of directors. The majority of the directors are professionals—prominent technocrats, philanthropists, and academics who serve a fixed three-year tenure. However, for the first time in the organization's short history, the current chairperson of the board is a politician of the ruling political party. A politician at the helm is indicative of the important role the foundation is playing in the provincial government's education roadmap. This not only signals government buy-in of the foundation's programmes, but also gives a degree of financial security to the foundation, which has been historically dependent on donor assistance.

Monitoring and Evaluation

Rigorous evaluations are built into BISP's design, including a dedicated unit for monitoring and evaluation. Evaluations are also undertaken by external organizations to enhance credibility. Invaluable insights are provided by these evaluations. To obtain a more balanced assessment of the organization's programmes, especially in the case of impact evaluations, both quantitative and qualitative analyses are undertaken. Three independent firms were hired to conduct spot checks of eligible beneficiaries, evaluate the processes of the programme in implementation, and carry out a detailed impact evaluation exercise.

Linked to this, an important strength of BISP has been its ability to learn from its mistakes and to strive for better mechanisms. For example, the shift from Phase 1 (identification of deserving recipients by elected representatives) to Phase 2 (poverty scorecard-based targeting) was based on learning the shortcomings of the first phase. Similarly, the disbursement of funds through Pakistan Post was abandoned once its weaknesses were realized, and there was a move to facilitate disbursements through smart cards, later through mobile phones, and finally through debit cards. At each stage, lessons were learned and were incorporated into the design of the programme.

A major reason for the success of the **Punjab Education Foundation** is its strong monitoring and evaluation department that not only continually inspects the functioning of various projects, but also provides regular feedback on how and where funds should be directed. PEF has a two-tier monitoring policy. While the monitoring and evaluation department oversees project performance from an administrative perspective, the Academic Development Unit helps regulate the quality of education being provided.

One of the major distinguishing features of the organization is its openness to change. Not only do the regulatory departments provide feedback, their reports are used by the board of directors regularly in the decision-making process. Successful programmes are put in the expansion phase while the less efficient ones are quickly discontinued. This dynamic nature of the organization ensures sustainable growth and success in the long-term.

Over time, the administration has shown a remarkable receptivity to change, and the board has been highly forthcoming regarding any actual or perceived weakness. Programme implementation is preceded by thorough evaluation via the initial pilot programmes, and less promising ventures have been readily discarded.

Rescue 1122 has a state-of-the-art, centralized monitoring, tracking, and evaluation system that seeks to ensure uniform quality of service delivery across Punjab. Through this system, the central control room maintains a steady flow of communication with emergency vehicles and substations. Possible instances of misuse of service or petty corruption are prevented through the use of a GPS-based fleet-tracking system that is equipped with a street-level map to assist with effective surveillance and fleet management. The institution's centralized tracking system involves a provincial monitoring cell that works in conjunction with district central rooms installed with internal and external cameras. In addition, an extensive call monitoring software is in place. The organization's wireless communications system 'serves as the backbone of the service' due to its indispensable role in the effective management of emergencies and disasters.

In the case of **LUMS**, a factor of importance is that outputs and outcomes are routinely measured and assessed. Some of the indicators measured are teaching evaluations, research produced and published in reputable journals, teaching material developed, case studies prepared, research funding generated, consultancy work undertaken, conferences attended, and training undertaken. All this is documented and reviewed annually and periodically at the school level by the Faculty Appointment and Promotion Committee (FAPC)/tenure committee, which makes decisions on the hiring and promotion of the faculty.

ROLE OF DEVELOPMENT PARTNERS

A critically important factor of success for organizations is the extent of significant and timely financial and technical support from external donors.

For instance, **LUMS** was considerably helped by the building of its well-designed and well-equipped current campus with a USD10 million donation from USAID in 1988—its first involvement with a private institution in Pakistan. It also received financial support from The Rausing Trust. More recently, LUMS has received generous grants from the Gurmani Foundation and UK's Department for International Development (DFID) which has helped enhance the scope of the National Outreach Programme.

Financial support for **IBA's** infrastructural development (upgrading of the existing facilities and new buildings) came largely from The Abraaj Group, The Aman Foundation, and Tabba Group. This timely support has laid a solid infrastructure base for adapting IBA's strategic development goals, improving teaching and research quality, and meeting expanded enrolment.

In 2009, **BISP** received a credit of USD60 million from the International Development Association (IDA) of the World Bank. It supported the design of the poverty scorecard, survey of all households in Pakistan, and related activities. The World Bank followed this up with an additional credit of USD150 million to launch the co-responsibility cash transfer for the primary school children of BISP's beneficiaries (*Waseela-e-Taleem*). USAID provided a grant of USD85 million as budgetary support for cash payments to the beneficiaries identified under the poverty scorecard system. Subsequently, USAID provided additional funding of USD75 million. In 2009, the Asian Development Bank provided a credit of USD150 million for use by BISP to make transfers to beneficiaries identified through the new targeting system. It followed this with a much larger credit of USD430 million. Finally, UK's Department for International Development (DFID) provided a grant of about USD450 million, equivalent to the conditional cash transfer for primary education of children of BISP beneficiaries. The reform of social protection has also figured prominently in Pakistan's negotiations with the IMF.

Additionally, BISP has been successful in developing and sustaining valuable partnerships with government as well as non-governmental and private organizations, including through sub-contracting arrangements. These organizations include NADRA, Pakistan Post, the Population Census Organization, commercial banks, survey firms, and mobile phone service providers. There are also emerging partnerships being developed with provincial governments. All these partnerships have facilitated the achievement of BISP's programme objectives.

To maintain world-class standards, **Rescue 1122** established the Emergency Services Academy—the first of its kind in Pakistan. Foreign experts visit the academy on a regular basis to train staff in the latest and most effective emergency services. To date, more than 7,000 rescuers have been trained.

Even though **Edhi Foundation** has strictly shunned foreign financial support (except from expatriate Pakistanis), it has been successful in establishing the necessary linkages with multiple agents at various levels involving both the public and private sectors in performing its duties. It works closely with other NGOs and with relevant government agencies and departments in responding to emergencies ranging from natural disasters to accidents and acts of terrorism.

ABILITY TO ADAPT TO CHANGING CIRCUMSTANCES

An important factor of success of institutions is their ability to adjust to existing and evolving challenges and opportunities. Institutions that fail to adapt to the prevailing environment are generally doomed to failure, whereas those that exhibit the ability to face unexpected changes are better positioned to be successful in their operations.

An important asset of **LUMS** has been its ability to adapt to prevailing circumstances. For example, the adoption of the case study method early on had a very positive effect on the curriculum. Similarly, there was a shift from the three-year undergraduate programme to the four-year programme after it was realized that foreign universities did not recognize the three-year programme. The rapid expansion of the university from a business school to four schools with varied disciplines is also indicative of institutional flexibility and ability to change.

Similarly, **NADRA** has exhibited a remarkable ability to adjust to, and take advantage of, evolving circumstances. A year after its establishment, it transformed the business model of registration based on manual data collection, followed by single data entry for automation. To ensure the integrity of the data, this was replaced by double entry of data. Second, to achieve greater financial autonomy in the face of perpetual fiscal constraints of the public sector, the agency decided to develop lucrative, value-adding in-house capabilities in areas such as data warehousing, project management, networking, and other areas which had previously been outsourced. Software development and integration was also undertaken within the agency. In the case of the biometric passport, the agency was venturing into hitherto uncharted territory. The entire technology was developed in-house. The organization took a calculated risk and succeeded. A more commercial, proactive and business-oriented approach pervades in the technical and management portions of NADRA. Risk-taking is encouraged. In many ways, these parts of the organization perform as if they were in the private sector in terms of entrepreneurial spirit. At the same time, the control systems are very tight and help in bringing visibility and transparency into processes and procedures.

This ability to adjust to changing environments is facilitated by the fact that some of these organizations exhibit remarkable receptivity to new ideas at all levels of management and staff. For example, **Rescue 1122** clearly stands out as an organization with the ability to adapt to challenging local conditions and constraints. Operating under a tight provincial budgetary allocation, Rescue 1122 does not have the luxury of making expensive mistakes. A city the size of Lahore would have required many more ambulances than the approved fourteen refurbished ones for the pilot project. In spite of this challenge, a carefully planned operation system and strategically located emergency units across the city resulted in the impressive response time of seven minutes. Since then, the organization has worked on an emergency response time model rather than a cost intensive population model. The latter would have entailed a much larger fleet of ambulances and a huge dent in the provincial exchequer. This is, therefore, an excellent example of efficient public sector service delivery which can be replicated across different services.

The expansion of Rescue 1122 in fire service is also an instructive case of low-cost adaptation to local conditions. The initial training of senior management, including Dr Rizwan Naseer, was in Glasgow, Scotland. Once trained, the management team helped train hundreds of local staff in the Rescue 1122 Academy. Moreover the organization has started indigenous manufacturing and repairing of emergency equipment and vehicles, saving millions of dollars in foreign exchange.

OTHER INDIVIDUAL FACTORS

In addition to the above groups of factors, there are some other factors, leadership qualities specific to the organizations that help underpin their success. The following are some examples.

LUMS and **IBA** admission policies have been strictly merit-based. At LUMS, students are selected through a rigorous process in which their academic potential, communications skills, intellectual prowess, leadership qualities, and commitment to hard work are assessed, For example, during the period 2000–2011, on average only 25 per cent of applicants for the BSc were selected. LUMS graduates continue to be hired by top companies in the country and the region, as well as in academia and government. A large number of its graduates are admitted in the masters and doctoral programmes of reputable universities in North America, United Kingdom, and Australia. Graduates of LUMS hold jobs in many countries.

Similarly, an important success factor for IBA has been its rigorous student selection procedures. The institute has always maintained a merit-based system, being selective in enrolment. For example in 2011–2012, some 2,250 students applied for the BBA, and only 469 (roughly 20 per cent) were selected. It has a strong disciplinary system, and examinations are always held on time, a remarkable achievement for an institution in strife-torn Karachi. To expand their horizons, students are offered exchange programmes with countries such as Malaysia, China, Singapore, and the United States. The good quality of IBA graduates and its strong alumni networks ensure relatively easy employability for IBA graduates.

In the case of **LUMS** and **Rescue 1122**, the institutions were able to establish early credibility, which helped in gaining legitimacy for them. The leadership of LUMS did not request the government for free land to construct the new campus. Instead, the leadership requested help in facilitating the adoption of its charter, which was made easier. In the case of Rescue 1122, the organization's early successes and rising popularity led to calls for expansion, and between 2005 and 2007, a fire brigade and water rescue service was started. The government's financial support followed the organization's ability to establish its credibility. Management has also succeeded in establishing an effective public relations campaign. Frequently, television advertisements were aired promoting Rescue 1122's image as Pakistan's premier emergency services organization, specifically emphasizing its response time of only seven minutes.

Sometimes, institutions succeed because they are filling an important lacuna. In the case of **IBA** and **LUMS**, the collapse of public higher education gave these institutions an opportunity to establish themselves as credible entities. Also on the demand side, there is a growing middle class in the country that can afford the tuition fees for their children at these institutions but not for their education abroad. There are also advantages of being an early entrant into the market. For example, Edhi and IBA were established in the early 1950s. **Edhi Foundation**, as one of the very first philanthropic organizations in Pakistan, filled a huge void in emergency and social services. Edhi started his ambulance service at a time when there was no other private ambulance service of note. Falling under the ambit of the Civil Defense Authority, the state of public emergency services was also fairly limited and rudimentary. Thus, Edhi helped fill a gap and soon became the largest ambulance service in the country. Similarly, upon its establishment in 1955, **IBA** was the first business school in Pakistan, and indeed was the first business school established outside of North America. This gave it a flying start, which carried it for almost thirty years without any competition in Pakistan. The institute fell on bad times during the late 1990s, but it has managed to recover since 2002 (see Chapter four).

Edhi Foundation has achieved popularity among all groups, especially minorities, because of its non-ethnic and non-sectarian approach. It is completely blind to differences in ethnicity, sect, or religion in the provision of social services within the society. This particular characteristic comes directly from the person of Abdul Sattar Edhi, who has infused these progressive values into the organization. In fact, the foundation has sometimes come under serious threat from fundamentalist groups because of its non-discriminatory, pluralistic, and progressive approach and policies.

Finally, in the case of **BISP**, a good grievance mechanism exists. Offices have been established at tehsil level, and internet access has been assured for grievance reporting. This has kept the system responsive to the concerns of the recipients. Spot checks are also carried out, and there is also a process evaluation mechanism.

It will be instructive to compare the factors for success of the above organizations with those of Pakistan's failing entities such as PIA and Pakistan Railway.

In the case of PIA, there has been massive political interference in hiring, resulting in major overstaffing: There are 19,500 employees for only 31 operational planes, that is, 630 employees/plane, compared to 245 for Emirates and only 70 for Turkish Airlines. There have been cases where sacked employees have been reinstated (Sacked Employees Reinstatement Act of 2010) when they were fired under the previous PML-N regime of 1997–1999.

Another problem for PIA has been the role of trade unions and the short tenure of its top management, on many occasions prematurely curtailed by the pressure of trade unions. Management's decision-making is frequently impaired by a plethora of trade unions. Even managing directors of the organization have been forced to resign.[4] Also, the practice of placing pilots as heads of the organization instead of experienced aviation management experts has weakened the management capabilities. The problem has been aggravated by the short tenure of top management.

PIA also suffers from being subjected to poor regulatory arrangements. CAA, the regulatory body for all airlines in Pakistan, has not been regulating PIA adequately. CAA lacks independence, and has been led by one or other of its clients, switching between head of CAA and PIA, with periods when the top manager held both positions.

In the case of **Pakistan Railway**, the factors for failure have been even more blatant. It is the largest public sector employer in Pakistan with over 80,000 employees. Frequently, PR cannot pay workers on time, with its gross earnings barely enough to cover salaries and wages. Its social welfare function seems to overwhelm its financial objectives. For example, the pension cost of PR in 2013–14 was about PKR15 billion, more than half of the payroll cost of employees. Because of overemployment, many workers stay at home, drawing their wages. Others perform clerical work, where they review and process no more than a single file in the course of an eight-hour shift.

PR also lacks autonomy and is subjected to significant political interference as a result of its financial dependence on the state. There is significant interference from the federal government, especially after the merger of its relatively independent Railway Board with the Ministry of Railways. The situation was aggravated further by the appointment as chairman of a civil servant in 1990, with no prior railway experience, nor knowledge of the sectoral issues relevant to PR. Thereafter, decisions increasingly became political, rather than being based on economic efficiency grounds. The creation of the National Logistics Cell (NLC) further reduced the demand for PR's services. The management of NLC is drawn mainly from the military and has, therefore, a great deal of clout in resource allocation and other decisions compared to PR.

Finally, PR has witnessed much mismanagement and lack of planning and direction. Departments such as revenue and expenditures work as 'silos' with minimal interdepartmental coordination and interaction. There is, therefore, little coordinated financial planning or analysis of the feasibility of train services and routes.

To summarize, there are specific factors that determine the success or failure of organizations. Those that succeed are marked by having clear objectives and goals, unencumbered by unrelated social objectives. They have financial autonomy and sustainability. They have a clear vision and continuity of leadership. They enjoy managerial autonomy and generalized political support. They have rigorous monitoring and evaluation systems in place which are built into the design of the programmes. For all these reasons, they are able to attract competent managers and staff who ably perform their functions. By contrast, failing institutions are subject to excessive government control, overstaffing, vague objectives, and excessive pressures from outside actors such as trade unions.

14

Remaining Issues and Challenges

As indicated in the previous chapters, the organizations included in this study have a good track record, despite the extremely unfavourable institutional environment in the country. These organizations are diverse in terms of their missions, objectives, and areas of coverage. Despite their success, however, these organizations have various remaining problems and challenges, which need to be addressed to make them even more successful. The purpose of this chapter is to summarize some of these issues.

Financial autonomy has been one of the hallmarks of most of these organizations. Its absence can be an issue for at least three of these organizations. In the case of **Shaukat Khanum Cancer Hospital**, its reliance for over half of its total revenues on donations puts its long-term financial sustainability at risk, particularly given the fragility of the country's economic situation and the foray of Imran Khan into party politics, which is bound to alienate at least some donors. Moreover, any large-scale expansionary programmes will necessitate funding on a much wider scale than currently afforded. Similarly, in the case of the **Punjab Education Fund**, there has been heavy reliance on foreign donors for its operations and investments. Since 2005, when the institution was restructured in line with World Bank recommendations, international donors (World Bank, Canadian International Development Agency (CIDA), and UK's Department for International Development (DIFD)) have provided a total of USD540 million. This high dependency on donor funding can challenge the institution's long-term financial sustainability. The provincial government and the board of directors of the foundation would have to come up with a viable financial strategy through which alternative sources of funding are tapped. A step in that direction has been taken by the provincial government which has allocated funds to the PEF in its annual development budget.

Likewise, in the case of **BISP**, international donors (primarily the World Bank, USAID, and Asian Development Bank) have provided a staggering amount of USD1.4 billion in financial support to the organization. Should the priorities for lending by these international agencies shift to other areas, BISP's financial sustainability could be severely jeopardized.

Another challenge that threatens future success is the uncertainty around the future leadership of some of these institutions. As already mentioned in earlier chapters, **Edhi Foundation's** success has, largely, been an outcome of the character and personality of its leader, especially because the organization is run in a very centralized way. The management structure entails few lines of authority between management and staff. There is no visible middle-level management in place, and high-level 'circle managers' run the day-to-day operations and collaborate directly with employees and customers. The circle managers are directly accountable to Edhi, and zonal offices are managed directly from the centre, allowing them limited autonomy. The philanthropist approves all projects personally, on a day-to-day basis, and retains the final say in all decisions from the most significant to the least. This strictly centralized system is a deliberate decision of Mr Edhi, who firmly believes that centralization of management, finances, and planning is the main reason for the organization's credibility, success, and growth. In recent years, owing to Edhi's ill health, the management of many affairs has been passed on to his family and to Dr Kazmi, a middle-aged professional, who continues to maintain Edhi's centralized management approach. Questions already abound about the foundation's fate after Edhi's demise, and while Edhi asserts that his three daughters and two sons will take command, without him at the helm, donors will be more reluctant to be as generous as in the past. In short, a more professional, decentralized and transparent system of organizational and financial management would need to be put in place in which decision-making is not vested in the hands of a few. Moving away from an individual-centric to a professional-management model would be imperative in preserving the credibility, reputation, and efficiency of the institution.

Another organization where future leadership is an issue is **Rescue 1122**. Dr Rizwan Naseer, an orthopedic surgeon by profession, has been able to transform the organization from a small-scale Lahore Pilot Project into an institution with operations spread across the Punjab province. The level of efficiency in service delivery has been achieved in large measure due to the considerable internal cohesion and dedicated teamwork nurtured by the resourceful Dr Naseer. Interestingly enough, he still retains much of the staff that assisted him with the organization's establishment a decade ago. Once again, the issue remains how the organization will evolve beyond the tenure of its present leader. The provincial government will need to establish a viable and credible process through which the organization can find an able successor to Dr Naseer. The government's continued support would also be needed in terms of budgetary provision and recognition of organizational autonomy, that is, a commitment not to interfere negatively in the workings of the organization. To some extent, the success, reputation, and popularity of the institution in terms of continued effective service delivery would itself garner political support—a virtuous circle of effective service delivery and political ownership.

The two educational institutions—LUMS (private) and IBA (public)—have their own set of challenges. In the case of **LUMS**, there are governance issues, specifically the role of the five- to six-member management committee. The best international universities exhibit shared governance with the academic community, in control of the essential academic decisions, and the managers and administrators responsible for resources, facilities, and other administrative matters. This has not always been the case with LUMS. There is need for the management committee to focus on strategic decisions, and to put in place criteria for measuring performance. Too often when tensions have arisen on tenure and resources, the committee has reacted by centralizing decision-making, which has made the situation worse. Moreover, the committee has no academics on it, depriving it of adequate representation of the views of the faculty. Tensions have developed between the committee and the vice chancellors, resulting in a high turnover of vice chancellors. For example, between 2001 and 2013, there were four changes of vice chancellors, a very high turnover compared to some reputable international universities.

IBA has its own problems. First, it needs to find a better balance between teaching and research. To be considered a successful research institution, IBA will need to place a greater emphasis on research, which carries important weight with the Higher Education Commission's (HEC) ranking criteria. IBA can be involved more actively in giving policy advice to the federal and provincial governments, as well as to the private sector in areas of its comparative advantage. In particular, the computer science faculty needs to cater more to the technological needs of the local industry. Now that the physical infrastructure and information technology base is well on its way to be completed, IBA needs to encourage and reward faculty members and students for quality papers published in top international journals in relevant fields.

A challenge, not of IBA's making, is the low degree of internationalization, which is also a benchmark for university rankings. For a number of reasons, most prominently the security situation in Karachi, the number of foreign faculty and students at IBA is negligible compared to the years prior to the 1980s when the institute attracted students and faculty from the United States, Malaysia, Australia, China, and the Middle East. For IBA to get international ranking, it must have at least 50 per cent international students. Efforts in that direction include sending students abroad and holding more events (conferences, seminars, fora, and symposiums) outside the country. Until there is a significant improvement in the security situation in Karachi, and more generally in Pakistan, this challenge will continue to remain.

There are other, more organization-specific, challenges. For example, in the case of **BISP**, while the PML-N government has continued the political support to the organization, a transition has to be made from excessively relying on leaders and champions to establishing a more solid institutional set-up that can weather political transitions. Thought should also be given to checking the excessively fast expansion of BISP into too many areas. It will be important that the programme remains focused on what is already being achieved. New activities should be undertaken on a pilot basis, and only when the feasibility for scaling up and resources (financial and human) are identified, should BISP expand into those areas.

For **Shaukat Khanum Cancer Hospital**, the most significant challenge is the availability and retention of high quality human resources. In particular, retaining qualified doctors with international experience is, perhaps, the most challenging aspect of administration and management in light of the unstable and precarious political and security environment in the country. So far, the institution has been relatively successful in meeting this challenge, but there is no guarantee for the future. Another factor that hinders the function and efficiency of the hospital is the energy crisis, which has stifled economic activity in the country for the past several years. The chronic energy crisis has also put a heavy burden on hospital resources, pushing its systems and finances to the limit. Alternative power generation has been put in place, but comes at a substantial running cost to the hospital.

For the **Punjab Education Foundation**, as gains from education accrue only over the long run, by their very nature, programme interventions in education are difficult to evaluate with much accuracy in the short-term. Since PEF runs multiple and simultaneous projects at any given time, monitoring becomes challenging, and in certain cases projects are monitored at random rather than at a regular basis.

Finally, in the case of the **Motorway Police**, the change in culture witnessed as compared to the other police services of the country is the result of dynamic leaders with foresight. It will be important to continue employing professional and experienced staff to head the organization. Also, foreign training of the organization's staff should be continued to improve overall performance and skills acquisition in techniques and management. Foreign training was a regular feature until a few years ago when it was discontinued for budgetary reasons.

Finally, as indicated earlier, **NADRA**'s key remaining challenges are institutionalizing policies, processes, and procedures so that decisions are taken not on a haphazard basis, but under a clearly laid out process. Also, while it is the role of leadership to manage political pressures, it is crucial that it does not get involved in party politics. On the government side, to whom the organization responds, efforts should be made to avoid political considerations in the hiring and firing of NADRA's top leadership.

15

Conclusion

In Pakistan's chequered history of the last sixty-eight years, the focus, too often, has been on the negative aspects of the country's economic and social development. This is understandable, given the endless woes of the citizenry amid mounting socio-economic problems. The country's development indicators are not only dismal, but have also deteriorated compared to other countries.

Despite this, there are candles in the dark environment of the country that shed light on another narrative. Amidst the hostile and fragile institutional environment of the country, there are organizations that are surviving well—thriving and meeting their stated objectives. This study selected nine such Pakistani organizations, cutting across all important sectors and of varying sizes and missions. Of course, these are not the only successful entities in the country.

The question this study has endeavoured to answer is: How are these organizations able to succeed in achieving their goals in an environment that is not conducive to growth and progress? In other words, how do these entities survive and thrive in the midst of major challenges and poor governance in the country's institutional structure?

The study identifies nearly a dozen factors responsible for the success of these organizations and illustrates how each one uses its coping mechanism to steer through turbulent institutional waters to reach their goals.

The study found that clarity and simplicity of mission and objectives is an important success factor. Organizations with clear, specific, and focused objectives and ones which are not encumbered with distracting responsibilities are more likely to succeed. By contrast, entities that are saddled with multiple and conflicting goals are handicapped in achieving their goals.

As with any enterprise in the world, a key ingredient in the recipe for success is strong and visionary leadership that is able to steer the organization through turbulent waters. This means a leadership that can define and implement a clearly articulated mission, that is able to assure the financial viability of the organization, and that is capable of buffering the organization against unnecessary outside intervention. It also helps if this capable leadership has sufficient continuity of tenure to transform objectives into results and institutionalize the standard processes and procedures. The study has enumerated several cases where leadership at specific moments in the life of these organizations has made a difference. In some cases, this leadership is ensconced in a group of senior managers, while in other cases, such as the Edhi Foundation, this is based in individual, charismatic leaders.

The best leadership is also one that deepens and strengthens institutions, and clearly lays down and codifies the policies, processes, and procedures of these institutions. A good example of effective institutional strengthening is IBA, where the Dean has clearly codified rules and procedures, based on which the relevant decision-making authority has been delegated to the faculty and administration. By contrast, NADRA, despite its good performance, has witnessed the 'founder's syndrome', with the fortunes of the organization closely linked to those of the previous chairman. Similarly Edhi Foundation leans very heavily on its aging founding father, with a question mark remaining on the future of the entity post-Edhi.

The success of organizations also depends on the competence and dedication of its managers and staff. The study concludes that a common characteristic of successful enterprises is their ability to recruit and retain competent staff who are given sufficient elbow room to perform their functions and pursue their initiatives. Putting in place rigorous and merit-based recruitment procedures and resisting pressures for politically-motivated filling of jobs are important ingredients of success. Exposing staff to international experience through well-designed training programmes certainly helps in this process.

Pivotal to the success of any organization is financial sustainability, the entity's ability to count on adequate and stable funding. Without this, the organization will be heavily dependent on government resources, and hence, subject to public interference in the daily activities of the entity. The study illustrates how various institutions have managed to achieve financial sustainability over time and have thus kept the government at bay.

Designing procedures, such that there is an arms-length arrangement between the owners (government or private sector) and the management, is a prerequisite for the successful implementation of day-to-day operations. Where ownership is too intrusive, despondency sets in and there is a high turnover of management, which frustrates the initiative of the managers and staff. In the case of government entities, widespread political support facilitates the work of the entities—support that can survive changes in government and the accompanying changes in management.

Putting in place robust monitoring and evaluation mechanisms to measure success and learn from experience is another important building block for success. The sample of case studies included here illustrate the importance of building evaluations into the design of the programmes. Such arrangements not only increase accountability based on clearly articulated benchmarks, but also provide opportunities to organizations to learn from mistakes. Learning organizations are invariably successful organizations.

Serendipity or proactivity can ensure external financial support to organizations. Significant and timely financial and technical support from external donors can provide the oxygen needed, especially during the formative years.

Specifically, institutions such as LUMS, BISP, and the Punjab Education Foundation have had their programmes boosted by sizeable external funding at appropriate times. On the other hand, excessive reliance on outside funds can blunt efforts to ensure long-term financial sustainability. And there are entities such as Edhi Foundation that specifically forego support from foreign donors (except from Pakistani expatriates) on grounds that this jeopardizes their legitimacy.

Finally, as with all organizations—private or public—the ability to adapt to changing circumstances is an important success factor. Institutions that fail to adapt to the prevailing environment are generally doomed to failure, whereas those that exhibit agility in facing unexpected changes are better positioned to be successful. Invariably, most organizations encounter such unexpected developments.

The nine enterprises included in this study are examples of successful enterprises, and the reasons for their success are summarized in the previous chapters. However, this does not imply that they do not have weaknesses. Indeed, these institutions have a sizeable agenda of unfinished business which needs to be addressed.

A key concern is the excessive dependence of some of these enterprises on external donor financing. Shaukat Khanum Cancer Hospital, Punjab Education Foundation, and the Benazir Income Support Programme all have heavy dependence on outside donors. This high dependency on donor funding can be a challenge to the long-term financial sustainability of these institutions.

Uncertainty around the future leadership of some of these organizations is also a concern. What happens to Edhi Foundation after the demise of the ageing Abdul Sattar Edhi? How will the operations of Rescue 1122 be affected in the absence of Dr Rizwan Naseer? BISP too needs to make a transition from dependence on leaders and champions to establishing a more sustainable institutional set-up that can weather political transitions.

Finally, many of these institutions suffer from problems which are not of their making. Foremost among these problems are those of security and terrorism, which have a debilitating effect on the domestic and foreign investment in these organizations. Similarly, the two higher education institutions reviewed in this study (LUMS and IBA) are failing to attract any foreign faculty or students. Two decades ago, this was not the case. Likewise, critical energy shortages are having a severe impact on most of these institutions. These problems are unfortunately expected to remain in the foreseeable future.

What are some of the lessons that emerge for policymakers, managers of public organizations, and international development partners?

First, the government should leave sufficient space for organizations so as not to stifle their initiative. There is nothing more distractive and destructive to organizations than meddling by public owners in the human resource and investment decisions of the enterprises. Rather than meddle in their day-to-day operations, the government should set benchmarks for organizations in terms of meeting agreed upon objectives and goals. Typical arrangements have included performance contracts between organization managers and their controllers.

Second, governments should make sure that the organizations under their purview have simple, but effective, monitoring and evaluation systems in place that provide a practical and empirical basis for assessing results (both outputs and outcomes). These systems are also excellent evaluative instruments to learn lessons from experience.

Third, governments should ensure that decisions on hiring and firing of top management are not taken capriciously or purely on the basis of short-term political considerations. Continuity of good leadership is important, and it should not be sacrificed at the altar of every change in government. As mentioned earlier, it takes at least a decade to get real traction for good performance. This involves defining unambiguous and easily implementable objectives and goals, building strong internal capabilities and external alliances, and proceeding with the implementation to the point of critical mass that resists reversal of progress made.

Fourth, following Levy's (2014) 'with the grain' approach, policymakers should utilize existing institutions to the maximum extent possible, instead of setting up new arrangements automatically in response to internal or external pressures. Efforts at reforming organizations should be in line with the country's political and institutional realities.

Finally, governments should not burden enterprises with extraneous and burdensome objectives that detract them from their core mission and objectives. If the government requires an enterprise to pursue an activity that diverges from its core functions, the government should compensate the enterprise up front in terms of financial and non-financial support.

On their side, organizations would do well to institutionalize policies and procedures so that there is no excessive dependence on the tenure of charismatic and individual-based leadership. This will avoid the uncertainty that surrounds changes of leadership. Even the most honest and visionary leadership cannot assure sustainability of organizations without institutionalization of operations and strategy so that the incoming leader can take over the reins from his/her predecessor.

Organizations can also help themselves by putting in place client-oriented systems. In this respect, putting in place a good grievance mechanism, such as that in place at the Benazir Income Support Programme, is a positive step in capturing feedback from clients and stakeholders and acting upon this feedback. Similarly, the cultural change effected in Pakistan's generally corrupt police service by the Motorway Police is at least partly a result of responding to and respecting motorists. It is heartening that the experience of Motorway Police is being expanded to other highways and motorways in the country.

Also, in a country where the media is so sensational and cynical, organizations should be prepared to take advantage of the media. It is important not just to do things but also to be seen doing them. A good example is Rescue 1122's successful television promotions, where it is highlighted as Pakistan's premier emergency services organization, with a clear and repeated emphasis on its response time of only seven minutes.

International development partners can also ensure success of public organizations by not imposing donors' priorities and deadlines on them. They should allow enterprises sufficient time and space to develop their programmes and take ownership of these. Too often, programmes fail because they are dictated to by donors, without full participation of national entities. Also, to the most extent possible, donors should employ the procurement, financial management, and reporting mechanisms of the country, while ensuring that the domestic institutional capacity is built to ensure efficient and transparent systems.

Work on these issues in developing countries is still in its infancy. There are only a handful of studies that explain 'pockets' of success in fragile institutional environments. Any follow-up to this study should expand its focus to more enterprises. These nine organizations are examples of success, but they are clearly not the only ones in Pakistan. There are many more success stories which also need to be highlighted and analysed. This study has also covered the experience of two failing institutions (PIA and Pakistan Railway). Examining other failing organizations can also help in drawing lessons.

Future work should also have a more geographical spread in coverage. All enterprises in our sample are headquartered in Lahore, Karachi and Islamabad. Future work should also include successful organizations from Khyber Pakhtunkhwa and Balochistan.

Notes

Introduction

1. This study uses a slightly adapted version of the methodology used by Barma (2013). It also draws on the work of Brinkerhoff (2005) and Leonard (2008).
2. See for example World Bank (2011); Pritchett and de Weijer (2010), and Fukuyama (2004).
3. Barma (2013).

Chapter 1

1. Pakistan Electronic Media Regulatory Authority (PEMRA), 2013.
2. Financial institutions (58%) and the judicial system (56%) also earned the trust of the majority of Pakistanis in the May 2011 survey. On the other hand, confidence in the national government (31%) and local police (32%) remained low. *Abu Dhabi Gallup Centre*, May 2011.
3. This question was earlier raised by North (1990) of why some economies develop institutions that produce growth and development, while other economies develop institutions that produce stagnation. North won the Nobel Prize for Economics for his work on institutions, De Soto (2000) has expressed a similar view. With a different perspective but still stressing the importance of institutions, Ferguson (2013) tries to explain why Western countries are in a decline while countries like China are forging ahead.
4. *Patwari* is a government official who keeps records regarding the ownership of land. *Thanedar* is a low-level policeman. The two officers are traditionally associated with petty corruption.

Chapter 2

1. This section benefited greatly from the discussion in Barma (2013).

Chapter 3

1. Interview with Mr Javed Hamid, 1 November 2013.
2. Research at LUMS, 2013. LUMS, Lahore.
3. HEC is a regulatory authority for higher education which provides guidelines, ranks universities, and provides partial funding.

Chapter 4

1. For example, the morning-MBA strength declined from 272 to 63 and from 307 to 248 for the evening MBA programme.
2. HEC is a regulatory authority for higher education which provides guidelines, ranks universities, and provides partial funding.

Chapter 5

1. Quoted by Express Tribune, 9 July 2013.
2. Based on interview with former Inspector General of Pakistan's Motorway Police, Mr Zia ul Hasan on 31 October 2013.
3. Hasan, Zia ul (2011): *Pakistan Motorway Police: A Success Story of Cultural Transformation.* Lahore, Pakistan.
4. Ibid.
5. World Bank (2002) Anti Corruption Strategy Report, Washington DC.

Chapter 6

1. Ms Farzana Raza was replaced as chairperson of BISP by Mr Enver Baig.
2. PML-N was in the coalition government headed by PPP when BISP was established.
3. Zakat payments are made biannually and Baitul Maal payments are made annually.

4. Also referred to as Co-responsibility Cash Transfer.
5. Based on an interview with an official of BISP on 20 November 2013.

Chapter 7

1. Jan (2006).
2. This section draws on Jan (2006).
3. See for example Ayub and Hegstad (1986).
4. Average age between 30–40 years for most functions except registration and vigilance. See Jan (2006).

Chapter 8

1. According to the Learning and Educational Achievement in Punjab Schools (LEAPS) survey, share of private schools in the Punjab increased from 15 per cent to 30 per cent.
2. Literacy rate in Pakistan is estimated to be about 50 per cent and for females it is 35 per cent. The net enrolment rate is 37 per cent for the poor and 59 per cent for those classified as non-poor (World Bank, 2002).
3. Interview with PEF management.
4. Interview with PEF management.
5. In Pakistan PPPs models range from adopt-a-school programme, concessions to private schools, public school up-gradation to school management committees, and citizen community boards.
6. Interview with PEF management.
7. Various studies have shown that distance to schools is one of the major impediments leading to low enrolment especially amongst girls in rural areas of Pakistan.
8. Interview with PEF management.
9. Ibid.
10. Interview with PEF management.
11. Ibid.
12. Ibid.
13. Ibid.

14. Ibid.
15. Interview with PEF management.
16. Ibid.
17. Ibid.
18. Ibid.
19. Ibid.
20. Ibid.

Chapter 9

1. The Marine Service has a total of twenty-eight rescue boats which provide aid and rescue missions in flood affected areas. These boats are also used to rescue people on the beach side of the Arabian Sea (from Edhi Foundation website).
2. A change in vision, goals, or strategy which may occur at all levels within the organization and where management may be able to perceive changes in noticeable factors relatively easily but might have difficulty in detecting changes in less obvious activities (Miles, 1978).

Chapter 10

1. The Punjab Emergency and Ambulance Services Pilot project 2004 was approved at the cost of PKR116,119 million.
2. The recruitment process was a written exam, psychological test, skill test, physical test, and a final interview. The organization has recently outsourced the recruitment to the National Testing Service (NTS) which does the initial screening of applicants—shortlisted candidates are subsequently interviewed in the 1122 academy.
3. Due to the absence of indigenous fire rescue training programmes, Dr Rizwan Naseer and some senior officers of Rescue 1122 had to receive training from the Glasgow (United Kingdom) fire rescue department. Since then fire rescue training is provided in-house at the Rescue 1122 Academy.
4. An example of this was the height rescue drill given to the first batch of employees. The drill entailed climbing a 100-foot tower

and rappelling down. In the absence of any trainers, Dr Rizwan Naseer himself volunteered to climb and rappel down the tower every day.

Chapter 11

1. Information in the case study comes from a series of interviews with SKMCH management and website.
2. Dr Faisal Sultan (transcribed interview).
3. From SKMCH and RC presentation, 2013.
4. Ilyas, Ferya. *PML-N harmed Pakistanis by attacking Shaukat Khanum: Imran Khan.* The Express Tribune, 2012. Web.

Chapter 12

1. Hussain, Abid (2015), 'Plane Truths', *Herald Exclusive*, March 2015.
2. Aijaz Haroon, Nadeem Yousafzai and Junaid Younis are three such examples.
3. Pakistan Civil Aviation Authority website http://www.caapakistan.com.pk/AboutUs.aspx.
4. Aviation Safety Network (ASN) database.
5. Hasan, Saad (2013), 'Sweeping Change: CAA, PIA and ASF Leave Ministry of Defence's Wings', *Express Tribune*, 10 June 2013.
6. Tahir, Nadia (2012), *Development and Efficiency: Analysis of Pakistan Railway in Comparison with China and India.*
7. Ibid.
8. Khan, Saad (2010), 'Pakistan Derailed', *The Huffington Post.*
9. Government of Pakistan (2013), Economic Advisor's Wing, Finance Division, *Pakistan Economic Survey.*
10. Ibid.
11. LUMS Case (2015), 'Pakistan Railway', *SDSB.*
12. Government of Pakistan (2013), Economic Advisor's Wing, Finance Division, *Pakistan Economic Survey.*
13. Ibid.

14. Kakakhel, Ijaz (2015), 'Railways Faces over PKR12 bn Deficit in First Five Months of FY 2014–15', *Daily Times*, 18 Jan 2015.

15. In the fiscal year 2013–14, the Government of Pakistan allocated PKR63.04 billion as part of the Public Sector Development Program (PSDP) to the National Highway Authority (NHA), while the allocation to Pakistan Railways was just PKR39 billion. Similarly in the fiscal year 2012–13, the government allocated PKR51 billion in PSDP to the NHA whereas it allocated only PKR23 billion to PR.

16. Siddiqa, Ayesha (2007), 'Military Inc.', *Inside Pakistan's Military Economy*.

17. Ibid.

18. Tahir, Nadia (2012), *Development and Efficiency*.

19. LUMS Case (2015), 'Pakistan Railway', *SDSB*.

20. Khan, Saad (2010), 'Pakistan Derailed', *The Huffington Post*.

21. At the time of writing this case, a railway bridge near Gujranwala collapsed, leading to the death of 14 people.

22. Khan, Fiaz Ahmed (2013), *A Research Paper on Pakistan Railways: Its Current Condition and Cause Based Solutions*.

23. Walsh Declan 2013), 'After Decades of Neglect, Pakistan Rusts in its Tracks'. *The New York Times*, 18 May 2013.

24. Ibid.

25. Ibid.

26. Khan, Fiaz Ahmed (2013), *A Research Paper on Pakistan Railways: Its Current Condition and Cause Based Solutions*.

27. LUMS Case (2015), 'Pakistan Railway', *SDSB*.

Chapter 13

1. For example, for the Shanghai Jiao Tong University, the tuition fees account for only 2 percent. In the case of University of Malaya, tuition fees cover only 3 percent of the operating budget.

2. The foundation does, however, benefit from state tax exemptions.

3. Although there are issues, discussed in Chapter 14.

4. For example, Aijaz Haroon, appointed MD in 2008, was forced to resign in 2011 by protests of Pakistan Airlines Pilots Association (PALPA).

References

Acemoglu, Daron and James Robinson (2012). *Why Nations Fail. The Origins of Power, Prosperity and Poverty*. New York, Crown Business

Altbach, Philip and Jamil Salmi (ed.) (2011). *The Road to Academic Excellence: The Making of World Class Research Universities*, Washington DC, World Bank

Ayub, Mahmood and Sven Hegstad (1986*). Determinants of Performance of Public Industrial Enterprises*. Washington DC, World Bank

Bano, M. (2008). *Public Private Partnerships (PPPs) As "Anchor" of Educational Reforms: Lessons for Pakistan*. UNESCO Web

Bari, F. and Cheema A. (2012). *Political Economic Analysis: Social Protection and the Benazir Income Support Programme*. Islamabad, DFID

Barma, Nazneen (2013). *Institutions Taking Root: Building State Capacity in Challenging Contexts*. Paper prepared for World Bank Workshop. Washington DC, World Bank

Barnett, William, Melvin Hinich and Norman Schofield (1993). *Political Economy: Institutions, Competition and Representation: Proceedings of the Seventh International Symposium in Economic Theory and Econometrics*. Cambridge. Cambridge University Press

Bellina, S., D. Darbon, S. Eriksen and O. Sending (2009). *The Legitimacy of the State in Fragile Situations*. Paris OECD DAC

Brinkerhoff, Derick (2005*). Organizational Legitimacy, Capacity and Capacity Development*. Maastricht. European Centre for Development Policy Management

Brummitt, C. (2010). "Ageing Philanthropist is Pakistan's Mother Theresa". Associated Press. Web

Cliffe, Sarah and Nick Manning (2008). Practical Approaches to Building State Institutions, in Charles T. Call and Vanessa Wyeth (eds.) *Building States to Build Peace*. Boulder, Lynne Rienner Press

Daland, Robert (1981). *Exploring Brazilian Bureaucracy: Performance and Pathology*. Washington DC University Press of America

Datta, A. (2009). Public Private Partnerships in India: A Case for Reform? Economic and Political Weekly, Web

De Soto, Hernando (2000). *The Mystery of Capital*. New York

Edhi, Abdul Sattar and Tehmina Durrani (1996). *Abdul Sattar Edhi: An Autobiography: A Mirror to the Blind*. Islamabad. National Bureau of Publications

Ferguson, Niall (2013). *The Great Degeneration. How Institutions Decay and Economies Die*. New York. Penguin Press

Ferner, Anthony (1998). *Governments, Managers, and Industrial Relations: Public Enterprises and Their Political Environment*. Oxford. Blackwell

Fisher, P. and Lundgren P. (1975). The Recruitment and Training of Administrative and Technical Personnel, in Tilly C. (ed.) *The Formation of National States in Western Europe*. Princeton. Princeton University Press

Fukuyama, Francis (2004). *State-Building: Governance and World Order in the 21st Century*. Ithaca. Cornell University Press

Gazdar, Haris (2013). *Political Economy of Social Protection Reform in Pakistan*. Collective for Social Science Research

Government of Pakistan (2013). *Brief on Income Support Programme and Social Safety Nets*. Islamabad

Government of Pakistan (2007). *National Social Protection Strategy*. Islamabad. Planning Commission

Grindle, Merilee (1997). Divergent Cultures? When Public Organizations Perform Well in Developing Countries. *World Development* 25(4): 481–495

Grosh, B. (1991). *Public Enterprises in Kenya: What Works, What Doesn't Work and Why?* Lynne Rienner Publishers: Boulder, Colorado

Grosh, M., C. del Ninno, E. Tesliuc and A. Ouerghi (2008). *The Design and Implementation of Effective Safety Nets for Protection and Promotion.* Washington DC, World Bank

Hasan, Zia ul (2011). Pakistan Motorway Police. A Success of Cultural Transformation. Mimeograph of a presentation. Lahore

Husain, Ishrat (2012). Retooling Institutions, in Maleeha Lodhi (ed.) *Beyond the Crisis State.* Karachi. Oxford University Press

Husain, Ishrat (1999). *The Economy of an Elitist State.* Karachi. Oxford University Press

Ilyas, Ferya (2012). PML-N Harmed Pakistanis by Attacking Shaukat Khanum. Express Tribune. Web

Institute Of Business Administration (Various Annual Reports)

Israel, Arturo (1987). *Institutional Development: Incentives to Perform.* Baltimore. John Hopkins University Press

Jan, Zia Ahmad (2006). Catalysts for Change: The Unique Culture Behind NADRA's Success—A Case Study. Paper presented at Pakistan's 10th International Convention on Quality Improvement, November 27–28, 2006. Lahore

Kabeer, N. K. Mumtaz and A. Sayeed (2010). Beyond Risk Management: Vulnerability, Social Protection and Citizenship in Pakistan. *Journal of International Development.* 229 (1–19)

Khan, Farakh (2012). *Pakistan's Failing Institutions.* Pakistan Tea House, 25 September 2012

Khan, S. N. and S. Qutub (2010*). Benazir Income Support Programme and the Zakat Programme: A Political Analysis of Gender*. Overseas Development Institute

Kumar, Krishna (2008). Partners in Education? Economic and political Weekly. Web

Lahore University of Management Science (Various Annual Reports

Lamb, Robert (2005). *Measuring Legitimacy in Weak States*. College Park. Centre for International and Security Studies

Lambert, R. (1993). The Structure of Organization Incentives. *Administrative Science Quarterly*. Web

Leonard, David (2010). Pockets of Effective Agencies in Weak Governance States. Where Are They Likely and Why Does it Matter? *Public Administration and Development 30, 91–101*

Leonard, David (2008). *Where are "Pockets of Effective Agencies Likely in Weak Governance States and Why?* Working Paper 306, Brighton, Institute of Development Studies

Levy, Brian (2014). *Working With the Grain: Integrating Governance and Growth in Development Strategies*. New York. Oxford University Press

Lindert, Kathy, Anya Linder, Jason Hobbs and Benedicte de la Brier (2007). *The Nuts and Bolts of Brazil's Bolsa Famila Programme*. Washington DC, World Bank

Malik, Iftikhar and Lucien Pop (2013). *Consolidating Social Protection. Pakistan Policy Note*. Washington DC, World Bank

Manor, James (2007). *Aid That Works: Successful Development in Fragile States*. Washington DC, World Bank

Materu, P., P. Obanya and P. Roghetti (2011). The Rise, Fall and Re-emergence of the University of Ibadan, Nigeria, in Altbach and Salmi (eds.), *The Road to Academic Excellence. The Making of World Class Research Universities*. Washington DC, World Bank

Miles, R. (1978). Organizational Strategy, Structure and Process. *Academy of Management Review.* Web

Niland, John (2007). The Challenge of Building World Class Universities, in Jan Sadlak and Nian Cai Liu (eds.) Bucharest. UNESCO-CEPES, *The World Class University and Ranking: Aiming Beyond Status.* Bucharest. UNESCO-CEPES

Nishtar, Sania (2010). *Choked Pipes: Reforming Pakistan's Mixed Health System.* Karachi. Oxford University Press

North, Douglas (1990). *Institutions, Institutional Change and Economic Performance.* Cambridge. Cambridge University Press

O'Leary, S., I. Cheema, S. Hunt, L. Carraro and Pellerano (2011). Benazir Income Support Programme Impact Evaluation. Baseline Survey Report. Oxford Policy Management

Owuso, F. (2006). On public organizations in Ghana: what differentiates good performers from poor performers? *African Development Review* 18:471–485

Pasha, Hafiz (1995). Political Economy of Higher Education: A Study of Pakistan. Pakistan Economic and Social Review. Web

Pritchett, Lant and Frauke de Weijer (2010). Fragile States: Stuck in a Capability Trap? Background Paper for *World Development Report 2011.* Washington DC, World Bank

Punjab Education Foundation (2014). *Punjab Education Foundation.* Web. http://www.pef.edu.pk

Reimann, B. (1974). Dimensions of Structure in Effective Organizations: Some Empirical Evidence. *Academy of Management Journal.* Web

Shafiq, M. (2008). *Designing Targeted Educational Voucher Schemes for the Poor in Developing Countries.* Indiana University

Shaukat Khanum Memorial Cancer Hospital and Research Centre (2014). *Shaukat Khanum Memorial Hospital and Research Centre.* Lahore. Web. http://www.shaukatkhanum.org.pk

Tendler, J. (1997). *Good Governance in the Tropics*. Johns Hopkins University Press: Baltimore

Teskey, Graham (2005). *Capacity Development and State Building: Issues, Evidence, and Implications for DFID*. London DFID

Waddock, S. (1991). *Social Entrepreneurs and Catalytic Change*. Public Administration Review. Web

Weatherford, M. Stephen (1992). Measuring Political Legitimacy. *American Political Science Review* 86 (1): 149–166

White, Leonard (1958). *The Republican Era: 1861–1890: A Study of Administrative History*. New York. Macmillan

Wilson, James (1989). *Bureaucracy: What the Government Agencies Do and Why They Do It*. New York. Basic Books.

World Bank (2012). *Fighting Corruption in Public Services*. Washington DC, World Bank

World Bank (2012a). *Project Paper on a Proposed Additional Credit and Restructuring in the Amount of SDR 96.7 Million to the Islamic Republic of Pakistan for the Scale-up of the Social Safety Net Project*. Washington DC, World Bank

World Bank (2011). *World Development Report 2011: Conflict, Security, and Development*. Washington DC, World Bank

World Bank (2002). *Anti-Corruption Strategy Report*. Washington DC, World Bank

Zaidi, Syed Akbar (1986). Issues in Pakistan's Health Sector. Islamabad. *Pakistan Development Review 25 (1986)*

Index